MILADY'S
Standard

Comprehensive Training for Estheticians
Student Workbook

Elizabeth Tinsley
Contributing Author

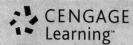
CENGAGE
Learning™

Australia Canada Mexico Singapore Spain United Kingdom United States

CENGAGE
Learning™

**Milady's Standard Comprehensive
Training for Estheticians
Student Workbook**

President:
Dawn Gerrain

Director of Editorial:
Sherry Gomoll

Acquisitions Editor:
Stephen Smith

Developmental Editor:
Judy Aubrey Roberts

Editorial Assistant:
Courtney VanAuskas

Director of Production:
Wendy A. Troeger

Production Coordinator:
Nina Tucciarelli

Channel Manager:
Sandra Bruce

Marketing Assistant:
Kasmira Koniszewski

For product information and technology assistance, contact us at
Cengage Learning Customer & Sales Support, 1-800-354-9706
For permission to use material from this text or product,
-0 submit all requests online at **cengage.com/permissions**
Further permissions questions can be emailed to
permissionrequest@cengage.com

Library of Congress Control Number: 2002023193

ISBN-13: 978-1-56253-805-7

ISBN-10: 1-56253-805-5

Milady
5 Maxwell Drive
Clifton Park, NY 12065-2919
USA

Milady products are represented in Canada by Nelson Education, Ltd.

For your lifelong learning solutions, visit **milady.cengage.com**

Visit our corporate website at **cengage.com**

Notice to the Reader

Publisher does not warrant or guarantee any of the products described herein or perform any independent analysis in connection with any of the product information contained herein. Publisher does not assume, and expressly disclaims, any obligation to obtain and include information other than that provided to it by the manufacturer. The reader is expressly warned to consider and adopt all safety precautions that might be indicated by the activities described herein and to avoid all potential hazards. By following the instructions contained herein, the reader willingly assumes all risks in con- nection with such instructions. The publisher makes no representations or warranties of any kind, including but not limited to, the warranties of fitness for particular purpose or merchantability, nor are any such representations implied with respect to the material set forth herein, and the publisher takes no responsibility with respect to such material. The publisher shall not be liable for any special, consequential, or exemplary damages resulting, in whole or part, from the readers' use of, or reliance upon, this material.

Printed in Canada
4 5 6 7 8 12 11 10 09 08

CONTENTS

HOW TO USE THIS WORKBOOK

This workbook is designed to accompany *Milady's Standard Comprehensive Training for Estheticians*. The exercises in each chapter, which follow the content in the textbook, are meant to test simple recall and reasoning and to reinforce your understanding of the information.

Exercises range from fill-in-the-blank questions to more challenging word puzzles, as well as discussion questions that encourage you to apply theoretical knowledge to real-life situations. You may wish to write your answers in pencil, either relying on your memory or consulting the textbook. Items may be corrected and rated during class or in discussion sessions with other students, or you may decide to use this workbook for independent study. After the last chapter there are two 100-item multiple-choice tests that allow you—without referring to the textbook—to test your grasp of the material and to identify those areas you may need to study further.

We hope you enjoy using this workbook and that it gives you a comprehensive, effective tool for learning about the world of professional skin care.

CHAPTER 1
A Journey through Time: Esthetics Then and Now

Date _____

Rating _____

Text pages: 3–23

Introduction

1. In the past, the beauty industry was dominated by _____ rather than skin care.

2. Modern esthetics uses a more _____ approach that integrates beauty, health, and wellness.

3. Antiaging body and facial treatments are aimed in particular at the _____ generation.

TOPIC 1: Career Options

1. Name positions for which a licensed esthetician would be qualified in a:

medical setting   _____

_____

_____

_____

department store   _____

_____

_____

magazine   _____

salon or day spa   _____

_____

_____

_____

TOPIC 2: Aesthetikos

1. The word *esthetics* comes from the Greek word _____ , which means _____

    _____ .

2. Explain briefly what an esthetician does. _____

    _____

3. Massage techniques performed by a massage therapist help alleviate or reduce _____ ,

    _____ , and _____ .

TOPIC 3: Ancient Surgery and Remedies

1. The early Egyptians, Romans, and Greeks were obsessive about _____ .

2. Ancient peoples used _____ , derived from the mignonette tree, to dye wigs, hair, and fabric.

3. Herbal remedies were often contained in authoritative books called _____ .

4. Match the following materials with their descriptions:

    _____ kohl   a. used for bathing, refining, and softening the skin

    _____ sour milk   b. used by soldiers to reduce sun glare

    _____ almond oil   c. derived from material related to arsenic and tin

    _____ lampblack   d. found floating in tropical seas

    _____ ambergris   e. rubbed on the body as a perfume

5. The holistic approach to wellness may be said to have begun with the Greek physician

    _____ .

6. Explain the basic philosophy behind the health practices of early Ayurvedic, Greek, Roman, and

    Chinese practitioners. _____

    _____

    _____

    _____

7. Louis Pasteur first proposed the theory that disease and infection were caused by

    _____ .

1. One theory of the origin of the word *spa* is that it is an acronym for the Latin phrase

    _____ .

2. Who was Fu Xi? _____

    _____

3. What is the difference between yin and yang? _____

    _____

4. Fill in the blanks in the sentences with terms from the following list. (Note that not all the

    terms are used.)

antibacterial	crimson	imbalance
chi	diurnal rhythms	qi
Chinese	Egyptians	toxic
circadian rhythms	essential oils	vermilion
cold cream	four humors	

   a. According to the Chinese, the cause of disease was _____ .

   b. Taoists believe that good health is based on the free circulation of a vital life force called

       _____ or _____ .

   c. _____ are the body's natural 24-hour cycle that, among other things,

       determine the times we sleep and awaken.

   d. The crushed plants and essential oils used in Hebrew health practices contained

       _____ properties that helped prevent disease.

   e. The _____ were the first people to develop distillation methods for extracting

       floral and herbal essences.

   f. Distillation is still the main method of extracting _____ .

   g. Blood, phlegm, yellow bile, and black bile were called the _____ by

       Hippocrates.

   h. Claudius Galenus was a Greek physician credited with creating the first _____ .

   i. _____ is a red pigment originally obtained by grinding cinnabar.

5. In addition to herbal cures, the Chinese used two other main treatments for the body. Name and describe them.

    a. _____

    _____

    b. _____

    _____

6. The Romans followed the traditions of the Greeks and Egyptians, but what are they best known for? _____

_____

7. _____ , called the science of longevity or science of life, was developed in ancient India. It is based on the belief that patients are responsible for _____

_____ .

8. The era after the fall of the Roman Empire, during which plagues and other diseases spread throughout Europe, is called the _____ .

9. Traditional African medicine is believed to be about _____ years old.

10. A skin-care ingredient that is derived from an African tree nut and still used today is _____ .

11. Describe beauty practices during the Victorian Age. _____

_____

_____

12. Vapor caves, steam baths, and cold-water bathing were characteristic of _____ practice.

13. Define *hydriatics*. _____

_____

TOPIC 5: Transition to Western Medicine

1. Compare the role of essential oils before the end of the 17th century and their role in the mid-20th century. _____

_____

_____

2. Western medicine is called _____ , which means that it focuses more on symptoms than on causes and does not accept treatments whose benefits cannot be proven scientifically.

TOPIC 6: Evolution of American Skin Care

1. In 1951, the discovery that water could penetrate the stratum corneum gave rise to the

_____ .

2. Match the following terms with their descriptions:

_____ Derma Analysis

a. introduced to the professional skin-care industry by Dr. Howard Murad

_____ CIDESCO

b. wrinkle cream developed by Ortho Pharmaceuticals

_____ Flexible Greasepaint

c. method for analyzing skin that is an industry standard

_____ AHAs

d. international organization that gives estheticians the opportunity to exchange experiences with colleagues

_____ Renova

e. ingredient used as household remedy for gunshot wounds, sunburns, and other lesions

_____ witch hazel extract

f. first makeup developed to make film actors appear more natural on screen

3. Match the following names with their achievements:

_____ Charles and Martin Revson

a. developed Flexible Greasepaint

_____ Christine Valmy

b. founded the Revlon Company

_____ Adrien Arpel

c. founded cosmetic and skin-care line using natural ingredients

_____ Aida Grey

d. first to introduce professional skin care to department stores

_____ Estée Lauder

e. developed concept of offering free gift with purchase

_____ Max Factor

f. opened the first esthetics school in the United States

TOPIC 7: Pioneers of the Twentieth Century

1. _____ was a French chemist who experimented with essential oils and believed they were more effective than their synthetic counterparts.

2. _____ used essential oils to help treat psychiatric disorders.

3. _____ established the first aromatherapy clinics in Paris, Britain, and Switzerland.

TOPIC 8: Emergence of Industry Conferences

1. During the late 1980s, as European and American skin-care companies introduced the latest products and technology at trade shows, what was true of the average esthetician or salon owner? _____

_____

_____

_____

2. How were the 1990s a "coming of age" for estheticians? _____

_____

_____

_____

Discussion Questions

1. How is the field of skin care changing and evolving?

2. What attracted you to the field of esthetics?

Word Review

aesthetikos	distillation	hydriatics	vermilion
ayurveda	essential oils	pharmacopoeias	yin and yang
CIDESCO	four humors	qi or chi	
circadian rhythms	henna		

CHAPTER 2
Anatomy and Physiology of the Skin

Date _____

Rating _____

Text pages: 26–49

1. Define *esthetics*. _____

_____

2. Name two reasons it is important for an esthetician to understand the basic principles of anatomy and physiology.

   a. _____

   _____

   b. _____

TOPIC 1: Skin Function

1. Adult skin may be described as follows:

   a. It weighs approximately _____ pounds.

   b. It is about _____ inches wide and _____ inches long.

   c. Each square inch contains approximately _____ feet of blood vessels, _____ feet of nerves, _____ sweat glands, and _____ oil glands.

   d. The skin contains more than _____ of all the blood in the body.

   e. The skin on the _____ is thickest; the skin on the _____ is thinnest.

2. List and describe the functions of the skin.

a. _____

_____

_____

b. _____

_____

_____

c. _____

_____

d. _____

_____

e. _____

TOPIC 2: Cell Physiology and Biochemistry

1. What are cells, and what is their main function? _____

_____

2. _____ are one-celled organisms with well-defined nuclei, no cell walls, and tail-like appendages, called flagella, that aid in movement.

3. Why is it important to understand basic cell functions? _____

_____

_____

4. The cell membrane is made of _____ and _____ and is permeable, meaning that _____ .

5. _____ is the ability of the cell membrane to allow some substances in while shutting others out.

6. Match the following cell parts with their descriptions:

_____ receptor sites   a. jellylike, watery fluid inside the cell

_____ ribosomes   b. cell structure containing DNA

_____ vacuoles   c. organelle that manufactures and holds protein for future use

_____ mitochondria   d. structures that store and transport water and ingested materials for future use

_____ cytoplasm

_____ nucleus

_____ lysosomes

_____ endoplasmic reticulum

_____ Golgi apparatus

e. receive signals from other parts of the body in the form of biochemicals and hormones

f. organelles that produce energy for the cell and manufacture ATP

g. series of small canals in the cytoplasm that allow substances to move in and out of cell organelles

h. organelles attached to the endoplasmic reticulum

i. structures that produce enzymes to help break down nutrients and break down the cell when it dies

7. The body uses amino acids to synthesize _____ .

8. Within the cell, nutrients and oxygen are used to manufacture _____ , a substance that provides energy to the cell and converts oxygen to _____ .

9. What is DNA? _____

_____

_____

10. Mitosis is _____ .

11. Characteristics such as brown eyes and a tendency toward oily skin are determined by

_____ .

TOPIC 3: Specialized Cell Function and Tissues

1. _____ cells have specific functions to carry out in the body.

2. Groups of cells that carry out the same function are called _____ .

   a. The skin is an example of _____ tissue, which is on the outside of the body's structures.

   b. _____ tissue lines the inside of the body and its organs.

3. Name and describe the three groups of muscles that make up muscle tissue.

   a. _____

   _____

   b. _____

   _____

   c. _____

   _____

4. What type of tissue:

   a. makes up the bones of the body?   _____

   b. connects the bones and provides a cushion between them?   _____

   c. includes blood and lymph?   _____

5. The flexible parts of the nose and ears are made of _____ .

6. Name the blood cells described:

   a. _____ are responsible for clotting

   b. _____ carry oxygen to body cells

   c. _____ help fight infection

   d. _____ are part of the immune system

7. What are the functions of lymph? _____

   _____

8. What is another term for fat tissue? _____

9. How do simple and stratified epithelium differ? _____

   _____

   _____

   _____

10. The epidermis is made up of _____ epithelium in layers.

11. Match these epithelial cells of the epidermis with their descriptions:

    _____ Langerhans   a. pigment cells

    _____ melanocytes   b. flattened cells at the skin's surface

    _____ Merkel cells   c. star-shaped immune cells

    _____ corneocytes   d. sensory cells

12. _____ in the dermis are responsible for forming collagen and elastin.

1. Fill out the crossword puzzle with the following clues:

Across

1. layer that connects the dermis to the epidermis
6. term for "many pores"
7. fat cells
8. oily substance produced by the sebaceous glands
10. fluid that fills empty spaces between collagen and elastin fibers
13. _____ apparatus; organelle that holds protein for future use
14. protein that makes up 70 percent of the weight of the skin
15. contains coding information that runs the cell
16. basic building block of the human body
17. process of cell division
18. live lower layer of the skin

Down

1. nerve endings that sense pressure or weight against the skin
2. lower part of the dermis
3. strong water-binder that helps retain fluid in the dermis
4. chief component of subcutaneous layer
5. common term for hair follicle
9. scar that results from overproduction of collagen
11. product of sudoriferous glands
12. _____ acids; proteins broken down in the cell

2. Fingerlike ridges called _____ form a membrane that attaches to the epidermis.

3. Collagen and elastin are injured by _____ .

4. Describe the subcutaneous or subcutis layer. _____

_____

5. _____ , formerly called Krause end bulbs, sense pain as well as pressure.

6. The _____ , the outermost layer of the skin, performs many immune and protective

functions.

   a. The _____ layer, formerly called the _____ , lies just above the

      papillary dermis. It is made of several layers.

   b. About 95 percent of the epidermis is made of _____ .

   c. Explain the process of keratinization. _____

      _____

      _____

      _____

      _____

   d. Name three functions of keratin. _____

      _____

   e. Above the basal layer is the _____ , also known as the spiny or prickle layer.

   f. What are desmosomes? _____

      _____

      _____

   g. The _____ contains grainy-looking cells filled with keratin.

   h. What are intercellular lipids, and what is their function? _____

      _____

      _____

      _____

   i. The structure of the epidermis has been compared to _____ .

   j. Define *barrier function*. _____

      _____

   k. Name the intercellular lipids that form the "mortar" in the epidermis. _____

      _____

      _____

l. Between the granular and outermost layers of the skin is the _____ , whose cells are filled with _____ , a substance involved in keratinization.

m. The outermost layer of the epidermis is the _____ , also called the _____ or _____ .

n. Mechanical or chemical exfoliation removes dead _____ from the skin's surface.

7. The hair follicle, technically known as the _____ , is commonly known as a _____ .

8. What causes clogged or enlarged pores? _____

_____

_____

9. Identify the skin and hair structures identified in the figure by writing their names in the corresponding spaces.

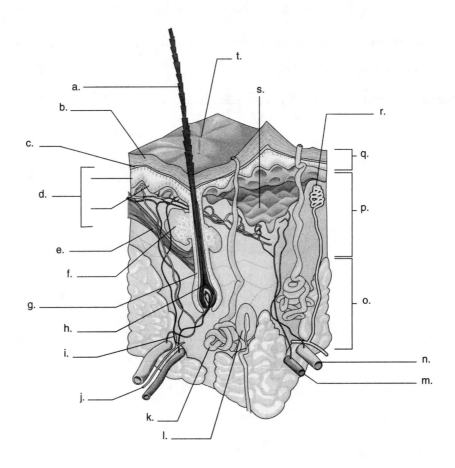

a. _____   k. _____

b. _____   l. _____

c. _____   m. _____

d. _____   n. _____

e. _____   o. _____

f. _____   p. _____

g. _____   q. _____

h. _____   r. _____

i. _____   s. _____

j. _____   t. _____

10. Sebaceous glands are not found in the:

    a. _____

    b. _____

    c. _____

11. The main function of sudoriferous glands is to _____ .

12. The main sweat glands are called _____ glands. The sweat glands in the groin and armpits are _____ glands.

13. Explain the function of melanocytes. _____

_____

_____

_____

14. The four colors found in the skin are _____ .

15. List and briefly describe the three types of melanin.

    a. _____

    b. _____

    c. _____

16. What is a tan? _____

_____

_____

17. Define *desquamation*. _____

_____

18. A surgical procedure called _____ can stimulate unwanted melanin production.

19. When too much melanin is produced in the skin, the result is _____ .

Discussion Questions

1. Why is it important that estheticians thoroughly understand skin anatomy? Cell anatomy?

2. Why is the dermis called the "live" layer of the skin?

3. Many people believe that a dark tan is not only attractive but completely harmless to the skin. How would you explain a tan to your clients?

Word Review

adenosine triphosphate (ATP)

adipose

adipose tissue

amino acids

barrier function

basal cell layer

cartilage

cells

ceramides

cholesterol

chromatin

collagen

connective tissue

corneocytes

cytology

deoxyribonucleic acid (DNA)

dermis

desmosomes

desquamation

differentiate

elastin

elastin fibers

eleidin

endothelial

epidermal strata

epithelial

esthetics

fatty acids

fibroblasts

glycosaminoglycans

Golgi apparatus

ground substance

hyaluronic acid

hyperpigmentation

immune cells

immune system

intercellular lipids

keloid

keratin

Langerhans

laser resurfacing

L-dopa

ligaments

lymph

lymph nodes

macrophage cells

mast cells

Meissner corpuscles

melanin

melanocytes

melanosomes

Merkel cells

mitosis

mucocutaneous corpuscles

nutrients

ostium, ostia

Pacinian corpuscles

papillae

papillary layer

phospholipids

pilosebaceous unit or apparatus

postinflammatory hyperpigmentation (PIH)

protozoa

rete pegs

reticular dermis

reticulin

Retin-A

ribosomes

sebaceous glands

sebum

selective permeability

sensory nerves

simple epithelium

stratified epithelium

stratified squamous epithelium

stratum corneum

stratum germinativum

stratum granulosum

stratum lucidum

stratum spinosum

striations

subcutaneous (subcutis) layer

sudoriferous glands

transepidermal water loss (TEWL)

tretinoin

CHAPTER 3
Body Systems

Date _____

Rating _____

Text pages: 50–67

Introduction

1. List the 10 systems of the body and the main functions of each.

a. _____

b. _____

c. _____

d. _____

_____

e. _____

_____

f. _____

g. _____

h. _____

i. _____

j. _____

_____

2. Identify the skeletal bones in the figure by writing their names in the following corresponding spaces:

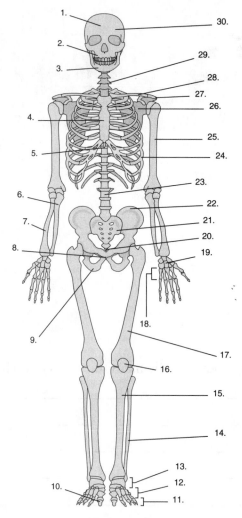

1. _____   16. _____
2. _____   17. _____
3. _____   18. _____
4. _____   19. _____
5. _____   20. _____
6. _____   21. _____
7. _____   22. _____
8. _____   23. _____
9. _____   24. _____
10. _____   25. _____
11. _____   26. _____
12. _____   27. _____
13. _____   28. _____
14. _____   29. _____
15. _____   30. _____

3. Identify the muscles of the body by writing their names in the following spaces:

1. _____

2. _____

3. _____

4. _____

5. _____

6. _____

7. _____

8. _____

9. _____

10. _____

11. _____

12. _____

13. _____

14. _____

15. _____

16. _____

17. _____

18. _____

19. _____

20. _____

21. _____

22. _____

23. _____

24. _____

25. _____

26. _____

27. _____

28. _____

29. _____

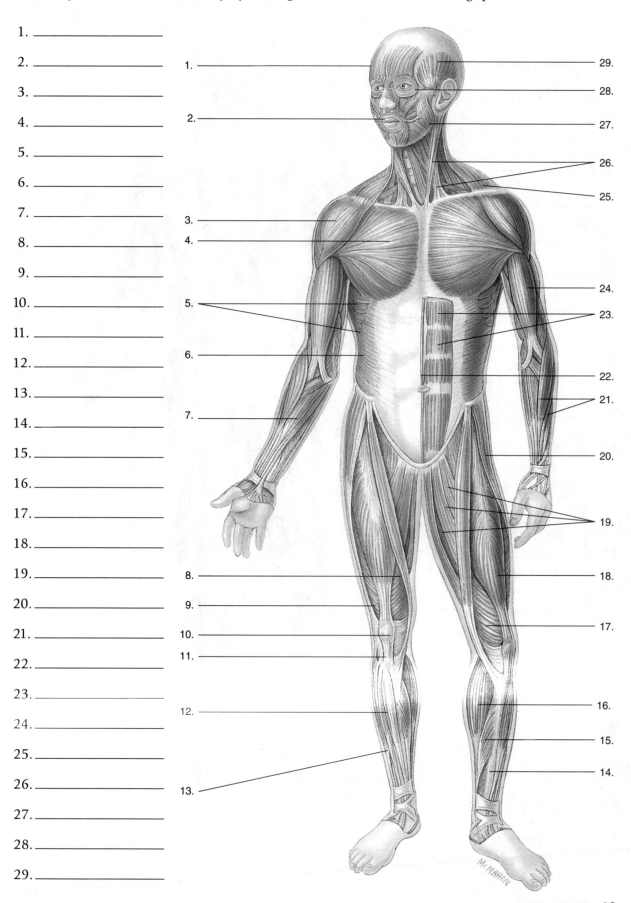

1. _____

2. _____

3. _____

4. _____

5. _____

6. _____

7. _____

8. _____

9. _____

10. _____

11. _____

12. _____

13. _____

14. _____

15. _____

16. _____

17. _____

18. _____

19. _____

20. _____

21. _____

22. _____

23. _____

24. _____

25. _____

26. _____

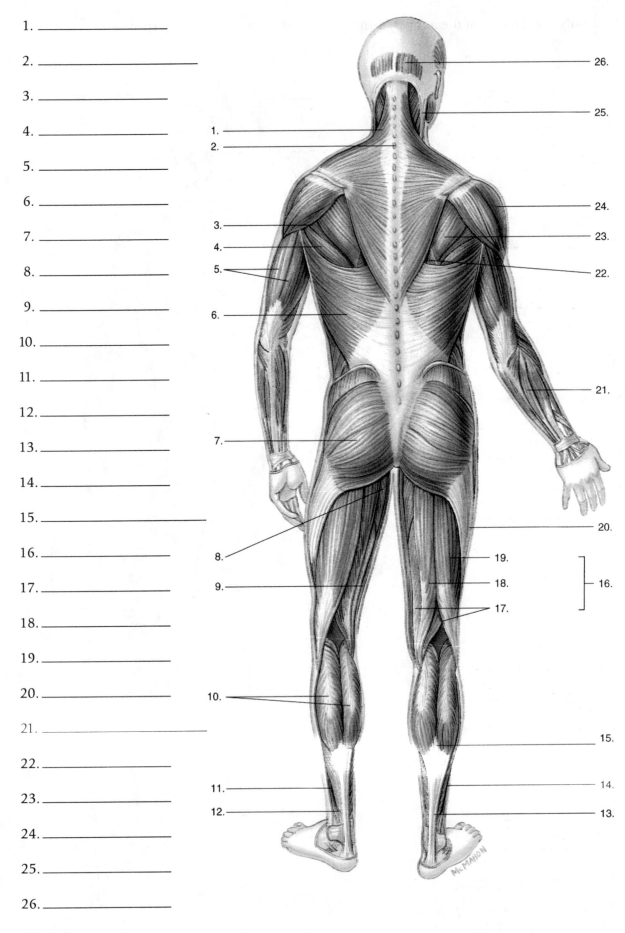

4. Identify the parts of the digestive system in the figure by writing their names in the following spaces:

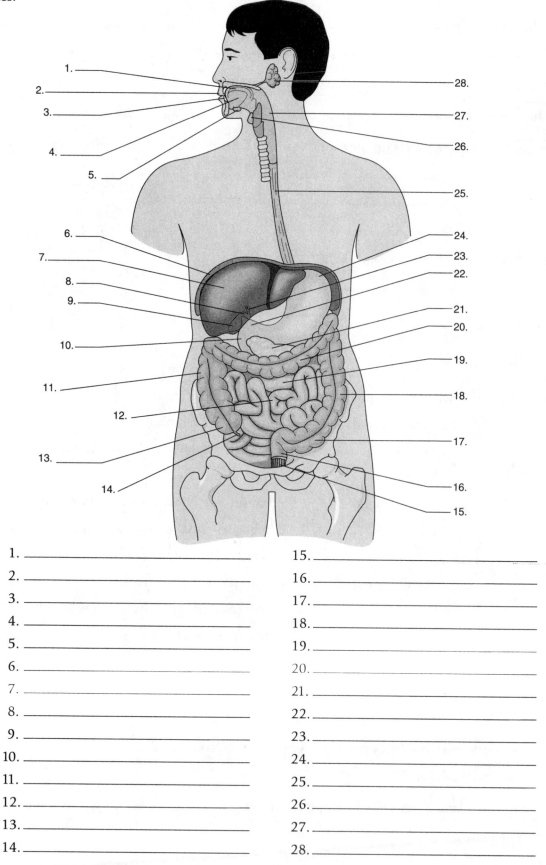

1. _____
2. _____
3. _____
4. _____
5. _____
6. _____
7. _____
8. _____
9. _____
10. _____
11. _____
12. _____
13. _____
14. _____

15. _____
16. _____
17. _____
18. _____
19. _____
20. _____
21. _____
22. _____
23. _____
24. _____
25. _____
26. _____
27. _____
28. _____

1. What are hormones? _____

_____

2. Male sex hormones, or _____ , are produced in the _____ .

3. The female sex hormones _____ and _____ are produced in the _____ .

4. Name some of the effects on the skin of overproduction or underproduction of sex hormones.

    a. _____

    b. _____

    c. _____

5. List four ways in which estrogen benefits the skin.

    a. _____

    b. _____

    c. _____

    d. _____

6. Match the following glands and hormones with their descriptions:

    _____ adrenal glands   a. produces T-lymphocytes

    _____ hypothalamus   b. located just above the kidney; secrete(s) cortisol and adrenaline

    _____ thymus gland   c. causes reactivity to stress and inflammation

    _____ adrenaline   d. regulates metabolism, heart rate, rate of energy used, and calcium

    _____ thyroid gland   e. stimulates the nervous system, raises metabolism, increases blood pressure to prepare the body for maximum exertion

    _____ pituitary gland   f. located at the base of the brain; coordinates hormone production

    _____ cortisol   g. ductless gland at the base of the brain

7. The adrenal cortex produces very small hormones called _____ or _____ that penetrate cells easily.

8. The thymus gland signals the development of the _____ in young adults.

TOPIC 2: Circulatory System

1. The circulatory system originates with the _____ .

2. Name and describe the three different types of blood vessels.

    a. _____

    _____

    b. _____

    _____

    c. _____

    _____

3. _____ capillaries deliver nutrient- and oxygen-rich blood to the tissues; _____ capillaries carry deoxygenated blood with carbon dioxide to the heart.

4. Identify the following arteries and veins:

    _____ largest vein returning blood to the heart

    _____ main artery that goes to the head and face

    _____ main artery coming out of the heart

    _____ vein between the anterior facial vein and the superior vena cava

    _____ artery supplying the upper cheek and facial sides

    _____ artery running diagonally from the corner of the eye across the nose

5. Fill in each blank with the correct term from the following list. (Please note that not all terms are used and that some are used more than once.)

arteries	lymph nodes	pus
carbon dioxide	lymphocytes	red blood cells
heart	nitrogen	veins
lungs	plasma	venous capillaries
lymph	platelets	

    a. When you cut your finger, _____ help stop the bleeding.

    b. The fluid portion of the blood is called _____ .

    c. _____ deliver oxygen to the cells and remove carbon dioxide.

    d. _____ defend body cells against disease.

e. The colorless fluid that bathes tissues and removes wastes and foreign bodies is

_____ .

f. The circulation of the blood may be described briefly as follows: The heart pumps blood to the _____ , where oxygen is picked up and _____ is removed. The blood then returns to the heart, where it is pumped out the other side through the _____ to the cells of the body. Cells deposit waste materials and carbon dioxide in the blood into the _____ , which goes into the veins through the _____ and returns to the _____ .

6. Unlike blood, lymph flows only _____ .

7. Where are the following lymph nodes located?

cervical nodes   _____

buccal nodes   _____

parotid nodes   _____

retroauricular nodes _____

8. What is the function of the thoracic duct? _____

_____

9. Lymph nodes are concentrated in the _____ , _____ , _____ , and

_____ .

10. Why is it important to have a basic understanding of the lymph system? _____

_____

_____

11. How is manual lymph drainage helpful before and after surgery? _____

_____

_____

Topic 3: Immune System

1. Why should an esthetician have a basic understanding of the immune system? _____

_____

2. Fill in the blanks in the sentences with terms from the following list.

antigen	lymph nodes	T-helper cells
autoimmune	macrophage	T-killer
B-cells	mast	T-suppressor
histamine	pseudopod	urticaria
hives		

a. A(n) _____ is a foreign invader, such as a bacterium or a virus, that could harm the body.

b. Langerhans have dendrites on one end and a _____ , or false foot, at the other. When they detect a foreign substance, they break off a piece and take it to a large immune cell called a _____ , found in the dermis and _____ . This cell gives off chemicals to signal white blood cells called _____ , which then signal the immune system in the bloodstream to react to the invader.

c. AIDS and lupus are considered _____ diseases because they result when the immune system directs the immune response toward the body's own organs.

d. Activated _____ cells kill invading organisms until another type of T-cell, _____ cells, signal the T-helper cells that the mission has been achieved.

e. Special memory cells called _____ recognize antigens from a previous illness and help the body respond more quickly to new attacks.

f. Hay fever, asthma, or bee stings activate a response by _____ cells, which secrete a chemical called _____ .

g. _____ , or _____ , is a swelling of the skin in response to an irritant or allergen.

Word Review

adrenal glands	aorta	estrogen	hypothalamus
adrenaline	autoimmune	external jugular vein	lupus
androgens	carotid	facial vein	lymphatic system
anterior facial vein	circulatory system	histamine	lymphocytes
antibody	digestive system	hives	manual lymph
antigen	endocrine system	hormones	drainage (MLD)

muscular system	pseudopod	superior temporal	thymus
nervous system	reproductive system	artery	thyroid gland
ovaries	respiratory system	superior vena cava	T-lymphocytes
pituitary gland	skeletal system	testes	transverse vein
plasma	superficial temporal	testosterone	urinary system
platelets	vein	T-helper cells	urticaria
progesterone			

CHAPTER 4
Bones, Muscles, and Nerves of the Face and Skull

Date _____

Rating _____

Text pages: 68–77

Introduction

1. For which salon procedures and situations is it important for the esthetician to know the anatomical structure of the face?

    a. _____

    b. _____

    c. _____

    d. _____

    e. _____

TOPIC 1: Bones of the Skull

1. There are _____ bones in the human body. Bone tissue is composed of:

    a. 1/3: _____

    b. 2/3: _____

2. List the functions of bones.

    a. _____

    b. _____

    c. _____

    d. _____

3. The skull consists of two parts: the _____ and the _____ .

4. Identify the parts of the skull in the figure by writing their names in the following spaces:

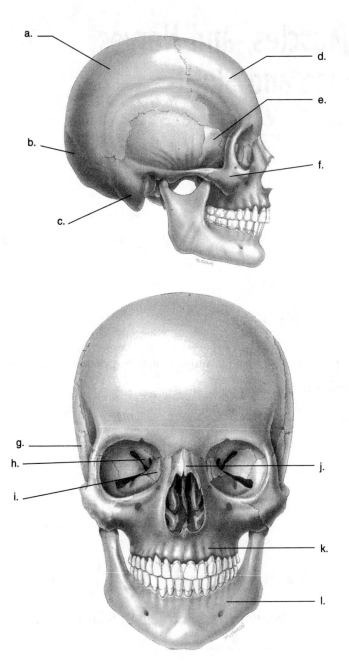

a. _____   g. _____

b. _____   h. _____

c. _____   i. _____

d. _____   j. _____

e. _____   k. _____

f. _____   l. _____

5. Identify the cranial and facial bones and write their names in the following blanks:

ethmoid bone	mandible	parietal bones
frontal bone	maxillae	temporal bones
lacrimal bones	occipital bone	

a. _____ upper jawbones

b. _____ forms the forehead

c. _____ lower back part of the cranium

d. _____ form the sides of the head in the ear region

e. _____ form the sides and crown of the cranium

f. _____ bone between the eye sockets

g. _____ form the sockets of the eyes

h. _____ lower jawbone

6. The technical name for the Adam's apple is _____ .

TOPIC 2: Muscles of the Face, Neck, and Scalp

1. Muscles compose about _____ percent of the body's weight.

2. Are facial muscles voluntary or involuntary? _____

3. Identify the muscles of the face and neck in the figure by writing their names in the following spaces:

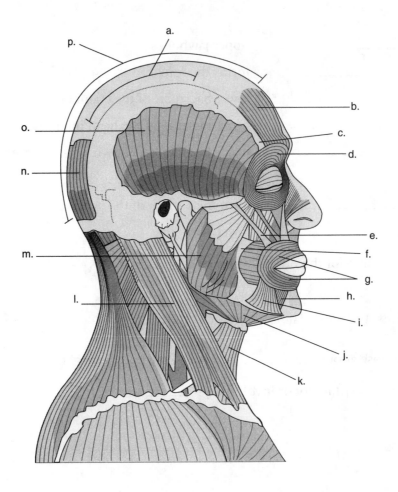

a. _____   i. _____

b. _____   j. _____

c. _____   k. _____

d. _____   l. _____

e. _____   m. _____

f. _____   n. _____

g. _____   o. _____

h. _____   p. _____

4. The small protein structures that make up muscles are called _____ .

5. The _____ is the end of the muscle that is attached to a stationary bone.

    a. The other end of the muscle, attached to a bone that moves, is the _____ .

    b. The central part of a muscle is its _____ .

6. Indicate in the following space where each of these muscles is located:

    a. _____ orbicularis oris

    b. _____ orbicularis oculi

    c. _____ occipitalis

    d. _____ pectoralis major

    e. _____ depressor anguli oris

    f. _____ sternocleidomastoid

    g. _____ zygomaticus major

    h. _____ deltoid

    i. _____ triceps

7. Identify the muscles described, using the following list of terms:

corrugator	masseter	sternocleidomastoid
depressor labii oris	orbicularis oris	zygomaticus major
digastric muscle	platysma	

    a. _____ makes the forehead scowl

    b. _____ attaches the mouth to the upper cheek

    c. _____ draws the corner of the mouth outward and backward, as in grinning

    d. _____ encircles the mouth

    e. _____ runs the length of the middle neck

    f. _____ connects the lower chin to the corners of the mouth

    g. _____ cordlike muscles on the front of the neck

    h. _____ responsible for firm chin and neck

8. Unscramble the terms for the muscles in the shoulder and arm and write them in the following spaces:

Scramble	Correct Word
roxlefs	— — — — — — —
	Clue: bend the wrist and draw the hand up
spiceb	— — — — — —
	Clue: located on the front of the upper arm
sneetsorx	— — — — — — — — —
	Clue: straighten the wrist, hand, and fingers
spritce	— — — — — — —
	Clue: covers the entire back of the upper arm and extends the forearm
proustian	— — — — — — — — —
	Clue: turns the hand outward, palm upward
cleptrasoi rajmo	— — — — — — — — — —
	— — — — —
	Clue: one of the muscles that cover the chest and assist in swinging the arms
toddeil	— — — — — — —
	Clue: large triangular muscle covering the shoulder
trasseur retinaro	— — — — — — — —
	— — — — — — — —
	Clue: assists in breathing and raising the arm
suzpraite	— — — — — — — — —
	Clue: one of the muscles that covers the back of the neck and upper/middle back
trooprans	— — — — — — — — —
	Clue: turns the hand inward, palm downward

TOPIC 3: Nerves

1. _____ nerves are responsible for feeling heat, cold, pain, and pressure. _____ nerves are responsible for movement.

2. What is the largest mass of nerve tissue in the body? _____

3. How many pairs of cranial nerves originate in the brain? _____ How many pairs of spinal nerves extend from the spinal column? _____

4. The main sensory nerve of the face is the _____ .

5. The main facial motor nerve is the _____ , also called the _____ .

6. Match each of the following nerves with its function:

_____ temporal   a. affects the midface and cheeks

_____ cervical   b. affects the jaw and lower face

_____ mandibular   c. controls the temples and forehead

_____ buccal   d. affects the eye area and forehead

_____ maxillary   e. affects the chin and lower jaw

_____ ophthalmic   f. affects the cheeks and upper jaw

7. Pressure or manipulation of _____ induces relaxation.

8. Identify the motor nerves in the figure by writing their names in the following spaces:

a. _____   i. _____

b. _____   j. _____

c. _____   k. _____

d. _____   l. _____

e. _____   m. _____

f. _____   n. _____

g. _____   o. _____

h. _____

Word Review

aponeurosis

biceps

Botox

corrugator supercilii

deltoid

digastric muscle

extensors

flexors

frontal bone

frontalis

hyoid

inorganic

latissimi dorsi

mandible

mastoid bone

maxillae

myofibrils

occipital bone

occipital frontalis

occipitalis

orbicularis oculi

orbicularis oris

organic

parietal bones

pectoralis

   major/minor

platysma

pronators

serratus anterior

sphenoid bone

sternocleidomastoid

supinators

temporal bones

temporalis

trapezius

triceps

zygomaticus

   major/minor

CHAPTER 5
Bacteriology and Sanitation

Date _____

Rating _____

Text pages: 78–89

Introduction

1. The _____ , or _____ , is the government
   agency that oversees workplace safety for employees.

TOPIC 1: Microorganisms

1. Germs that cannot be seen with the naked eye are called _____ .

2. _____ microorganisms do not cause disease. _____ microorganisms cause
   disease.

3. What are the shapes of the following bacteria?

   a. cocci   _____

   b. bacilli   _____

   c. spirilla _____

4. Which bacteria cause the following diseases?

   a. abscesses and boils _____

   b. tuberculosis   _____

   c. blood poisoning   _____

   d. syphilis   _____

   e. pneumonia   _____

5. Identify the bacteria illustrated in the following figure:

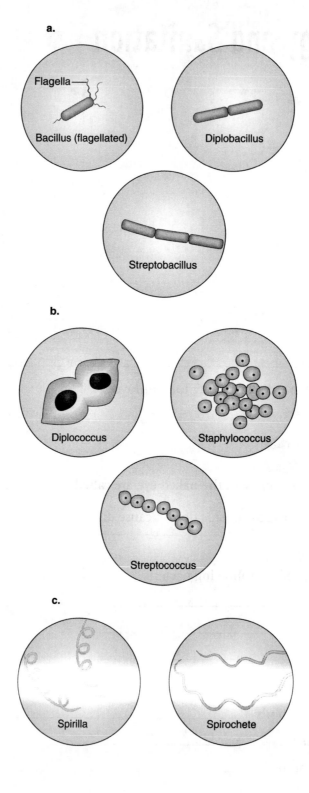

a.

Flagella

Bacillus (flagellated)

Diplobacillus

Streptobacillus

b.

Diplococcus

Staphylococcus

Streptococcus

c.

Spirilla

Spirochete

a. _____

b. _____

c. _____

6. Inactive bacteria can form protective outer shells and are then called _____ .

7. Yeasts, molds, and mildew are types of _____ .

8. Define the term *virus*. _____

_____

9. AIDS and hepatitis are both caused by _____ viruses.

TOPIC 2: Sterilization

1. To kill all bacteria, viruses, fungi, and bacterial spores, a surface or an implement must be

   _____ .

2. A device that uses very high heat and pressure to kill all microorganisms is a(n) _____ .

3. Why is it inadvisable to sterilize glass electrodes in an autoclave? _____

4. How do sterilization and disinfection differ? _____

_____

5. During disinfection, objects are immersed in chemicals called _____ agents.

6. To disinfect implements and equipment in the salon or spa, you should use _____
   _____ that kill _____ and _____ .

7. Because disinfectants can be very irritating to the skin, _____ may be used instead.

8. Items used in esthetic procedures are either disposable or nondisposable. Sponges, paper
   towels, and esthetician's gloves are considered _____ . Linens, plastic spatulas, electrodes, and mask brushes are considered _____ .

9. What is a sharps box? _____

_____

10. Implements should be immersed in 1:1000 quat solutions for how long? _____
    _____ How long should they be sterilized in an autoclave? _____

11. Hydrogen peroxide in _____ percent solution can be used to clean the skin and minor
    cuts.

12. A tool or product with microorganisms in or on it is _____ . Touching a client's
    skin and then dipping the fingers into a cleansing product results in _____ .
    Instead, products should be removed from their containers with _____ .

13. Any object exposed to blood or bodily fluids must be _____ or _____ .

14. It is important that the esthetician wear _____ during all skin treatments.

15. What is an aseptic procedure? _____

_____

_____

16. Using the following words and phrases, fill in the blanks to describe the steps of an aseptic procedure. (Note that not all words in the list are used.)

a clean towel	cups	plastic wrap
another clean towel	discarded	rinsed
clean or sanitized	disinfected	sharps box
closed trash container	disinfected or sterilized	spatulas
consultation	electrolysis	vinyl
cotton	extraction	washed or sanitized
covered laundry receptacle	jars	waxing
or hamper	latex	

a. Before beginning any service, lay out all the implements you will need on _____ _____ and cover them with _____ .

b. Be sure to use only _____ linens, gown, and headband or cap for each client.

c. Hands should be _____ after touching a client's hair.

d. Put on _____ or _____ gloves before every treatment and wear them throughout. This is particularly important during and after _____ , _____ , and _____ .

e. Products should be removed from their containers using pumps, squeeze bottles, or disinfected _____ , or, better yet, dispensed into small, disposable _____ .

f. After the treatment, linens should be placed in a _____ , disposables should be discarded in a _____ , sharps should be placed in a(n) _____ , and reusable items should be _____ .

g. All surfaces touched during the treatment should be _____ .

17. Another sanitizer sometimes used in the salon is the _____ , which uses ultraviolet light.

TOPIC 3: Policies and Procedures

1. Fill in the following blanks, then find the terms in the word search puzzle.

   a. Workstations should be disinfected with a(n) _____ -grade disinfectant.

   b. To disinfect laundry during washing, add _____ bleach.

   c. Trash receptacles should be made of a(n) _____ material that can be sanitized.

   d. If sinks and showers are not well sanitized, _____ and _____ may grow around seals and drains.

   e. Ventilation systems in showers and wet rooms should be able to remove _____.

   f. Grout that is not _____ is a good place for mold or mildew to grow.

   g. Manicure and hair areas in a salon or spa should have their own _____ systems because of the chemicals involved in these services.

   h. Inadequate ventilation can lead to the transport of _____ and _____ through the salon.

   i. Information about a product, such as flammability, hazards, uses, and storage requirements, is contained in a(n) _____ .

   j. Salons are required by the government agency _____ to educate their employees about employee safety.

P	A	C	A	S	W	M	L	I	Y	K	H
A	N	E	H	B	S	Y	G	V	L	M	K
T	O	F	A	L	L	E	R	G	E	N	S
H	N	U	G	A	O	N	A	M	Z	R	H
O	P	V	M	O	W	R	O	L	S	X	Y
G	O	Y	Y	S	E	L	I	X	E	D	Z
E	R	U	X	H	D	X	V	N	R	D	S
N	O	I	T	A	L	I	T	N	E	V	W
S	U	L	A	T	I	P	S	O	H	L	P
K	S	T	E	A	M	G	L	X	Y	V	S
Z	S	L	A	D	A	P	X	Q	I	W	S

Discussion Questions

1. Why is it so critical that sanitation measures be followed exactly and in every case? What may result when sanitation is practiced carelessly?

2. How can you demonstrate to your clients that you are conscientious about their safety?

Word Review

airborne micro-
   organisms

antiseptics

aseptic procedure

autoclave

bacilli

benzalkonium
   chloride

bloodborne viruses

cocci

contaminated

contamination

cross-contamination

diplococci

disinfection

fungi

gloves

glutaraldehyde

hospital-grade
   disinfectant

host cell

isopropyl alcohol

Material Safety Data
   Sheet (MSDS)

microorganisms

mildew

mold

mycoses

nonpathogenic
   microorganisms

Occupational Safety
   and Health
   Administration
   (OSHA)

pathogenic micro-
   organisms

quaternary ammo-
   nium compounds
   (quats)

sanitation

sharps boxes

spatulas

spirilla

spores

staphylococci

sterile

sterilization

streptococci

wet sanitizing agents

viruses

yeast

CHAPTER 6
Nutrition

Date _____

Rating _____

Text pages: 90–103

TOPIC 1: Macronutrients

1. Macronutrients are defined as _____ _____ and include _____ , _____ , and _____ .

2. An adult body is composed of about 60 percent _____ .

3. Proteins, which are chains of _____ , are used in the duplication of _____ , which contains all the information body cells need to function.

4. Nonessential amino acids are those _____ . Essential amino acids must be derived from _____ .

5. What do carbohydrates do? _____ _____

6. Name and describe the three basic types of carbohydrates.

   a. _____

   b. _____
   _____

   c. _____
   _____

7. Match each of the following terms with its definition:

_____ monosaccharide   a. basic unit of a carbohydrate

_____ polysaccharide   b. two molecular sugar units

_____ glucose   c. one-unit sugar molecule that all cells use for energy

_____ disaccharide   d. chain of sugar unit molecules

8. Name three ways in which the body uses fats, or lipids.

a. _____

b. _____

c. _____

9. Why is linoleic acid called an essential fatty acid, and why is it important to our health?

_____

_____

10. _____ are the main fat in foods.

11. Hydrogen atoms attach themselves to the carbon atoms in fatty acids in a process called _____ , forming _____ .

12. Calories are a measurement of _____ .

13. In the ideal diet, less than _____ percent of calories should come from fats, and only _____ percent from saturated fats.

14. Meats and dairy products contain _____ fats; monounsaturated and polyunsaturated fats come primarily from _____ .

15. There is evidence that _____ acids increase the "bad" type of cholesterol and contribute to heart disease.

16. Cholesterol is found only in _____ .

17. A type of fat present largely in cold-water fish is _____ , which may decrease the clogging potential that leads to _____ .

18. In the blank before each of the following nutrients, write the letter corresponding to the nutrient type: P=protein, C=carbohydrate, F=fat.

_____ carrots

_____ eggs

_____ oat bran

_____ lard

_____ fish

_____ linoleic acid

_____ dried apricots

_____ black beans

_____ corn oil

_____ skim milk

TOPIC 2: Micronutrients: Vitamins

1. _____ are necessary for nutrients to be broken down in the body and for amino acids and fatty acids to be reconstructed as needed.

2. Vitamins A, D, E, and K are _____ vitamins. The B vitamins and vitamin C are _____ vitamins.

3. _____ are converted to actual vitamins once in the body.

4. In the blank before each of the following descriptions, write the name of the corresponding vitamin: A, B1, B2, B6, niacin, folacin, B12, biotin, pantothenic acid, C, D, E, or K.

_____ plays important role in synthesis of hormones, cholesterol, and phospholipids

_____ required for collagen production

_____ produced in intestinal tract by "good" bacteria

_____ also called riboflavin

_____ sunshine vitamin

_____ B vitamin important in mental health

_____ important in the metabolism of proteins and the production of such chemicals as histamine

_____ required for the manufacture of steroids and red blood cells in the body

_____ necessary for good eyesight, especially night vision

_____ antioxidant found in avocados, wheat germ, egg yolks, and safflower oil

_____ plays an important role in proper blood coagulation

_____ removes carbon dioxide from cells and converts carbohydrates stored as fat

_____ deficiency causes pernicious anemia

5. Vitamin A is a fat-soluble vitamin formally known as retinol.

   a. What is betacarotene? _____

   b. What are good sources of vitamin A? _____

   _____

   c. What can vitamin A deficiency cause? _____

   _____

   d. Skin drugs that use derivatives of vitamin A are known as _____ . An example is Retin-A, which is used to treat _____ and _____ .

6. Vitamin D is another fat-soluble vitamin.

   a. When exposed to sunlight, the skin synthesizes vitamin D from _____ .

   b. Dietary sources of vitamin D are _____ .

   c. What is the main function of vitamin D? _____

   _____

   d. What can vitamin D deficiency cause? _____

   _____

7. Vitamin E is also known as _____ .

   a. Vitamin E's primary role in the body is as an _____ , a substance that protects the body from damage caused by _____ .

   b. What are good sources of vitamin E? _____

   _____

   _____

8. Vitamin K is found in _____ . Deficiency causes

   _____ .

9. Why must the body have regular supplies of the water-soluble vitamins? _____
_____
_____

10. Fill in the blanks from the following list of terms. (Please note that not all terms are used.)

amino acids	fat	pernicious anemia
ascorbic acid	fatty acids	proteins
barrier function	folacin	pyridoxine
beriberi	glucose	riboflavin
biotin	niacin	stunted growth
carbon dioxide	pantothenic acid	thiamine

a. Vitamin B1 is also called _____ . Its role in the body is to remove _____

from cells and to convert carbohydrates stored as _____ . Deficiency causes

_____ and _____ .

b. Vitamin B2, or _____ , is used by cells to manufacture amino acids and fatty

acids.

c. Pellagra is caused by a deficiency of _____ , a vitamin found mostly in

_____ .

d. _____ , or vitamin B6, is closely connected to protein synthesis.

e. A deficiency of _____ can result in mental problems, birth defects, and colorectal

cancer.

f. Deficiency of vitamin B12 causes a disorder known as _____ .

g. _____ is involved in energy formation by cells and the synthesis of proteins and

_____ .

h. _____ plays a role in the synthesis of cholesterol and phospholipids,

which make up an important part of the _____ of skin.

11. Vitamin C, or L-ascorbic acid, performs many functions in the body.

a. Vitamin C is an _____ , protecting the body from problems caused by free

radicals.

b. List some of the functions of vitamin C.

_____

_____

_____

_____

_____

_____

c. A deficiency of vitamin C may cause _____ .

TOPIC 3: Minerals

1. Fill in the crossword puzzle using the following clues:

Across

4. involved and present in DNA and energy release

7. regulates water levels and the transport of materials through cell membranes

8. aids in healing; necessary for healthy digestion and metabolism

10. required for prevention of tooth decay and in muscle movements

Down

1. joins with vitamin C to form elastin

2. supplied by iodized table salt and shellfish

3. important component of red blood cells

5. required for energy use, water balance, and muscular movement

6. gives strength to keratin

9. required for formation and maintenance of teeth and bones

TOPIC 4: How Much Nutrition Do You Need?

1. The calorie intake for an adult male should be about _____ per day; for an adult female calorie intake should be about _____ .

2. Carbohydrates should account for _____ percent of all calories; protein should account for about _____ percent.

TOPIC 5: Nutrition and Esthetics

1. Name the only three ways to lose weight.

   a. _____

   b. _____

   c. _____

Word Review

antioxidants	fluoride	pantothenic acid	rickets
arteriosclerosis	follicular keratinosis	pellagra	selenium
biotin	glucose	pernicious anemia	sodium
calcium	hydrogenation	phosphorus	thiamine (vitamin B1)
carbohydrates	L-ascorbic acid	polysaccharides	tocopherol
cellulose	(vitamin C)	potassium	triglycerides
chromium	linoleic acid	prostaglandins	vitamin A (retinol)
copper	magnesium	proteins	vitamin D
disaccharide	manganese	retinoids	vitamin E
fats (lipids)	monosaccharide	riboflavin	vitamin K
fiber	omega-3 fatty acids	(vitamin B2)	zinc

CHAPTER 7
Room Furnishings

Date _____

Rating _____

Text pages: 106–115

TOPIC 1: Facial Chair

1. The most important piece of equipment in the treatment room is the _____
   _____ .

2. The facial bed should be comfortable for both practitioner and _____ .

TOPIC 2: Operator Chair or Stool

1. An operator's stool that is _____ is healthy for the spine.

2. What is treatment rhythm, and why is it important? _____
   _____
   _____
   _____

3. To assist clients in safely getting on and off the facial bed, provide a _____ .

TOPIC 3: Maintenance of Furniture, Equipment, and Countertops

1. Keep the following considerations in mind when caring for equipment:

   a. Before cleaning tools and equipment, check with the _____ .

b. Avoid using _____ cleansers such as ammonia, scouring powders, window cleaner, and harsh solvents.

c. Upholstery made of _____ is particularly susceptible to damage from oils and heat.

TOPIC 4: Ergonomics

1. The ideal operator's stool has a(n) _____ backrest.

2. When performing a facial:

   a. Wear comfortable shoes with _____ heels.

   b. Keep the client's head at the level of your _____ .

   c. Keep your hands at a _____ angle during facial massage.

3. An esthetician's uniform should provide good mobility in the _____ and _____ areas.

4. To prevent injury, it is wise to rest the hands periodically and to perform _____ to maintain flexibility.

TOPIC 5: Utility Carts

1. To organize supplies, products, and equipment, a _____ is necessary.

2. What is a back bar? _____

_____

Word Review

back bar   ergonomically correct   treatment rhythm

CHAPTER 8
Technological Tools

Date _____

Rating _____

Text pages: 116–135

TOPIC 1: Skin Analysis Equipment

1. A magnifying lamp, or _____ , uses a cool _____ lightbulb shaped like a ring.

2. A lamp's power of magnification is measured in _____ . For most estheticians, a lamp standardized at _____ suffices.

3. What is a Wood's lamp, and how is it used? _____

_____

4. What is the esthetician's role in diagnosing skin disorders? _____

_____

_____

5. For a Wood's lamp to be effective, the room must be _____ .

6. Skin scopes use a _____ light that penetrates the epidermis, helping the esthetician identify various skin conditions through different _____ .

7. Handheld skin scanners allow the esthetician to _____

_____ .

8. Match the following colors, as seen through a skin scope, with the skin conditions they indicate:

_____ light violet   a. horny layer, dead cells, dandruff

_____ yellow   b. thick corneum layer

_____ brown   c. thin skin, lacking moisture

_____ blue-white   d. sun damage

_____ bright fluorescent   e. dehydrated skin

_____ white spots   f. normal healthy skin

_____ purple fluorescent   g. hydrated skin

_____ white fluorescent   h. comedones

TOPIC 2: Skin-Care Machines

1. Rotary brushes are used to cleanse the skin and _____ .

2. Before the rotary brush is applied to the skin, it is dipped in _____ . It is then applied with _____ pressure, beginning at the forehead.

3. After rotary brush attachments are cleansed manually, they should be immersed in a _____ _____ .

4. The vacuum in a vacuum machine serves two purposes, which are to:

   a. _____

   b. _____

5. The rotary brush is not recommended for _____ or _____ skin. The vacuum should not be used on skin with _____ .

6. The spray attachment on a vacuum machine is generally filled with _____ . Spray mists have a _____ and _____ effect on the skin.

7. Name five benefits of steaming the face.

   a. _____

   b. _____

   c. _____

   d. _____

   e. _____

8. The antiseptic properties of steam mist are due to the presence of _____ .

9. When preheating a steamer, direct it _____ the client.

10. Using a steamer for too long may dry the skin because the skin _____ .

11. A steamer should be placed about _____ inch(es) from the face.

12. How can essential oils or herbs be incorporated into the steaming process? _____

_____

_____

_____

13. Certain precautions are critical to operating a steamer safely and keeping it in good condition:

    a. Use only _____ water inside the steamer.

    b. At the end of the day, _____ the jar and let it dry.

    c. When steamers are not cared for, _____ are likely to build up on the heater element.

    d. To clean a steamer, use a solution of _____ .

14. What is a Lucas sprayer? _____

_____

15. Which skin types benefit from treatment with a Lucas sprayer? _____

_____

16. The rapid oscillation of high-frequency current creates a _____ effect on the skin.

17. List six benefits of high-frequency machines.

    a. _____

    b. _____

    c. _____

    d. _____

    e. _____

    f. _____

18. Neon gas inside an electrode produces _____ light. Argon produces

_____ light.

19. In each of the following spaces, write the corresponding type of electrode: mushroom, indirect (spiral), sparking (glass tip), or comb (rake).

_____ ideal for sallow and aging skin

_____ helps disinfect and heal acne lesions

_____ commonly used for normal to oily or sensitive skin

_____ may be used in scalp treatments

_____ skin contact must be maintained throughout the procedure

_____ may be used with cream and gauze for a facial finish

20. Before an electrode is removed from direct contact with the skin, the esthetician must

_____ .

21. A galvanic machine converts _____ current to _____ current. In skin treatments it is used to produce two reactions: _____ .

22. Define disincrustation, and explain how it is used. _____

_____

_____

23. During the process of disincrustation:

a. an _____ solution is applied to the skin

b. the client holds the electrode in a _____ polarity

c. the esthetician makes direct contact with the disincrustator set on _____ polarity

d. the process changes sebum in the skin to _____ , a process called _____

24. Disincrustation should only be applied to parts of the skin that are _____ .

25. What is iontophoresis? How is it used in skin treatments? _____

_____

_____

26. The process of iontophoresis is based on the universal laws of _____ .

a. During iontophoresis the electrodes must be _____ .

b. Products with a slightly acidic pH are considered _____ , while those with an alkaline pH are considered _____ .

c. If a product is negative, it should be applied with the electrode set at _____ .

d. The infusion of a positive product is called _____ ; the infusion of a negative product is called _____ .

27. Identify the pole that causes the following reactions by writing P for positive pole or N for negative pole in each of the following spaces.

_____ calms nerve endings

_____ causes acid reaction

_____ stimulates nerve endings

_____ decreases blood circulation

_____ causes alkaline reaction

_____ increases blood circulation

28. Electrodes should never be cleaned in a(n) _____ .

29. The ionto mask can be used in _____ or _____ .

TOPIC 3: Microcurrent Machines

1. Briefly describe the effects of microcurrent on facial muscles.

a. _____

b. _____

c. _____

_____

d. _____

e. _____

f. _____

2. What do wave therapy devices mimic? _____

_____

3. In wave therapy, motor nerves are stimulated to the point at which _____ .

4. In the past, motor nerves were stimulated with _____ current.

5. The _____ helps determine the strength of the current and the length of penetration.

TOPIC 4: Other Tools and Accessories

1. The purpose of a warm paraffin mask is to _____ .

2. Hot towels are warm, soothing, and softening to the skin and are ideal for removing

_____ .

3. A heat mask uses _____ heat and is placed on top of a(n) _____

_____ . As with treatments using galvanic current, the mask

causes _____ .

4. When a heat mask is used, treatment with a _____ or _____ is unnecessary.

5. Boots and mitts apply heat to the skin of the hands and feet to encourage _____ in the

torso and face, promote overall _____ , and restore natural _____ .

6. To meet sanitation standards, boots and mitts must be used with _____ .

7. Explain the process of microdermabrasion. _____

_____

_____

8. For which skin conditions is microdermabrasion recommended?

   a. _____

   b. _____

   c. _____

   d. _____

   e. _____

9. Microdermabrasion is *not* recommended for clients with:

   a. _____

   b. _____

   c. _____

   d. _____

10. How are lasers used in esthetics? _____

_____

_____

Word Review

anaphoresis	iontophoresis	microdermabrasion	waveform
cataphoresis	loupe	saponification	wave therapy
diopter			

CHAPTER 9
Basics of Electricity

Date _____

Rating _____

Text pages: 136–145

Introduction

1. The atoms and molecules that make up all matter are held together by _____ energy.

2. The production of electricity is based on the law of _____ .

3. Chemical electrical signals travel back and forth along the _____ to the _____ .

TOPIC 1: Basis of Matter: The Atom

1. An atom is composed of tiny particles called _____ and larger particles called _____ , which comprise protons and neutrons.

2. Negatively charged electrons orbit the positively charged _____ in an atom.

3. A hydrogen atom, which has one positive proton and one negative electron, is in a state of _____ .

4. The outermost ring of electrons in an atom is called a(n) _____ .

5. _____ electrons are difficult to move from their orbits; _____ electrons are easier to move.

6. How are ions formed? _____

_____

_____

_____

7. When two or more molecules are linked by an ionic bond, they form a _____ .

8. A water molecule is made of two _____ atoms and one _____ atom.

9. An electric current is a flow of _____ along a conductor.

10. Define the term *electric fields*. _____

_____

11. Copper is an example of a conductor, which can be defined as _____

_____ .

12. A material or element that does not easily pass an electrical current is a(n) _____ .

13. In each of the following spaces, write the term that matches the description.

covalent bond	hertz	proton
electric charge	kilowatt-hour	resistance
electric circuit	neutron	static electricity
electromagnetism		

_____ subatomic particle in the nucleus with a positive electric charge

_____ electric charge that is not moving

_____ amount of electric energy a 1,000-watt device uses per hour

_____ subatomic particle in nucleus that has no electric charge

_____ basic force in the universe that involves electricity and magnetism

_____ material's opposition to the flow of electric current

_____ path an electric current follows

_____ basic feature of certain particles of matter that causes those particles to attract or repel other charged particles

_____ the sharing of electrons between two atoms

_____ rate at which reversal of direction occurs in alternating current

14. Complete the crossword puzzle using the following clues:

Across

4. unit used to measure a material's resistance to the flow of electric current

5. material that easily passes an electrical current or flow of negatively charged electrons

6. unit that measures the rate of energy consumption, including electric energy

9. negatively charged particles that orbit the positively charged nucleus of an atom

10. control that regulates the strength of current

Down

1. piece of metal, glass, or other conductor through which current enters or leaves an electrical device

2. material or element that does not easily pass an electrical current

3. measured push or rate at which a current is being delivered

7. unit that measures the rate of flow of an electric current

8. atom or group of atoms that has gained or lost electrons and so has an electric charge

TOPIC 2: Circuits

1. In a lightbulb, the filament glows because it has _____ and gets hot; the wiring underneath has _____ and does not get hot.

2. The spark sometimes created when you touch a metal object, especially on a dry day, is an example of _____ .

3. Electrons moving in only one direction create a _____ .

4. Direct current produces _____ in the process called electrolysis.

5. The electrons in _____ current flow first in one direction, then in the reverse direction. This type of current is defined as _____ .

6. Why should an esthetician have a basic understanding of electricity? _____

_____

_____

TOPIC 3: Safety

1. All esthetic machines must comply with the U.S. _____ .

    a. All wall outlets should be the _____ type.

    b. A(n) _____ is not recommended, because it may fail to ground the machine properly.

    c. Well-made machines generally have _____ that automatically shut off the machine in case of a problem.

Discussion Questions

1. Name all the different ways in which you use electricity in a salon or spa, including uses not directly related to providing esthetic services.

2. How does a basic understanding of electricity help you select the proper treatment for each client? How does it help you provide safe and comfortable service?

Word Review

ampere	covalent bond	hertz (Hz)	ohm
bound electrons	electric fields	insulator	sinusoidal
circuit	electrons	ions	state of equilibrium
conductor	free electrons	molecule	voltage

CHAPTER 10
First Impressions: Setup and Supplies

Date _____

Rating _____

Text pages: 146–159

TOPIC 1: Elements of Meet and Greet

1. To create a professional appearance, estheticians should take a(n) _____ _____ approach.

2. Part of welcoming a first-time client should be a _____ , which can take an extra 15 or 20 minutes.

3. Taking extra time with new clients gains their loyalty, puts them at ease, and lays the foundation for the esthetician's _____ .

4. Why is it important to assess the client's personality and see that client as a whole person?

_____

_____

5. List the five Rs that will help you give your clients consistent and effective service.

   a. _____

   b. _____

   c. _____

   d. _____

   e. _____

6. How does a facial gown differ from a robe? _____

_____

_____

TOPIC 2: Facial Bed Setup

1. List and briefly describe the linens and other items used in cocoon draping, in the order in which they are placed on the facial bed:

   a. _____

   b. _____

   c. _____

   d. _____

   e. _____

   f. _____

   g. _____

   h. _____

   _____

2. Describe two ways of folding a towel around a client's head.

   a. _____

   _____

   b. _____

3. How does noncocoon draping differ from cocoon draping? _____

_____

_____

4. Which type of head covering is made of a light, meshlike material and is large enough to cover the ears and hair? _____

5. Can paper sheets and gowns replace cloth linens? Why or why not? _____

_____

TOPIC 3: Supplies

1. Fill in the blanks in the sentences from the following list of terms. (Please note that not all terms are used.)

cotton pads	palettes	sponges
cotton-tipped swabs	pumps	sterilized
disposable	rolls	tongs
fan	round	
gauze pads	sanitize	

a. Swabs, cotton pads and strips, eye pads, and condiment cups are considered _____ supplies.

b. Cotton _____ are less expensive than processed cotton balls.

c. _____ are commonly called "4 by 4s."

d. Small _____ brushes are useful for applying a product carefully and quickly, while small _____ brushes are good for applying makeup.

e. Estheticians can customize facial products and control the amounts of products they apply by using _____ .

f. All back-bar containers should have _____ with which to dispense products.

g. Once you have touched the client's skin, you should remove disposable items from their containers with _____ .

h. One advantage of stainless steel bowls is that they are easy to _____ .

i. Esthetic sponges must be _____ after each use.

j. Lipstick and eye makeup should *not* be removed with _____ .

TOPIC 4: Product Masks

1. Product masks target various skin conditions.

a. Pads soaked in a calming solution, such as _____ , are placed on the eyes _____ the mask is in place.

b. Masks are generally left on the face for _____ minutes.

c. Masks are removed with cotton squares or sponges moistened with _____ , beginning at the _____ .

TOPIC 5: Dispensary

1. Extra supplies and bulk products are usually kept under lock and key in a _____ .

2. Briefly describe two methods of setting up and using a dispensary. List the advantages and disadvantages of each method.

    a. _____

    _____

    Advantages: _____

    Disadvantages: _____

    _____

    b. _____

    _____

    Advantages: _____

    _____

    Disadvantages: _____

    _____

TOPIC 6: Safety

1. An important safety consideration before and after a treatment is helping the client _____ _____ .

2. To avoid accidents, spills should always be _____ .

3. Overheating facial and massage creams in a microwave oven may cause them to _____ .

4. Clean laundry should be folded and stored in _____ .

5. In most salons and spas the esthetician is required to leave the treatment room _____ _____ .

Word Review

dispensary

model

CHAPTER 11
Skin Types and Conditions

Date _____

Rating _____

Text pages: 162–169

Introduction

1. _____ refers to characteristics of the skin that are genetically inherited.

2. Skin is characterized as dry, normal, or oily depending on its _____ .

TOPIC 1: Skin Types

1. List the five categories in the professional system of skin typing.

   a. _____

   b. _____

   c. _____

   d. _____

   e. _____

2. In each of the following spaces, write the letter(s) corresponding to the skin type: N=normal, NC=normal-combination, DD=dry/dehydrated, OP=oily/problem, S=sensitive.

   _____ pore size appears to be enlarged

   _____ oilier T-zone

   _____ lacks water or oil

   _____ flushes easily and may feel uncomfortable when touched

   _____ may be irritated by perfumes and preservatives

_____ rare skin type

_____ treatment goal is to increase moisture or lipids/oil

_____ less inclined to form fine lines and wrinkles

_____ goal is to postpone aging with good cleansing and balance maintenance

_____ facial creams with higher water content recommended for this type

3. What are the characteristics of normal skin? _____

_____

4. In combination skin, the T-zone is oilier and shows more _____ , while other areas
   are _____ .

5. Briefly describe the treatment for normal-combination skin. _____

_____

_____

6. The lack of water in dehydrated skin may result from extrinsic damage, such as _____
   _____ , or intrinsic damage, such as _____ .

7. _____ skin lacks oil.

8. The aging process involves a decrease of _____ between the skin cells.

9. The first step in treating dehydrated skin is _____

_____ .

   a. The treatment goal for dehydrated skin is to _____ .

   b. Products used in this treatment should include those that _____

   _____ .

10. Treatment for dry/alipidic skin includes _____ facials and home-care products contain-
    ing both _____ and _____ .

11. It is possible for young, old, oily, or sensitive skin to suffer from _____ .

12. Using the words in the following list, fill in the blanks in the following sentences. (Please note that not all terms are used and that some may be used more than once.)

bacteria	hormonal	sallow
breakouts	hydrating	sebum
dead cells	moisture barrier	shiny
drying	oil production	thick
exfoliation	overcleansed	thin
flaking	puberty	

a. Oily skin is defined as having an excess of _____ or _____ .

b. Oily skin appears _____ , _____ , and _____ .

c. Follicles are clogged by clumping _____ and _____ .

d. Oily skin is at greater risk of _____ and is affected by such age factors as _____ and _____ fluctuations.

e. One advantage of excess oil is that it provides a better _____ , which prevents water loss.

f. If oily skin is _____ , the body may respond by producing more oil to compensate for the oil loss.

g. Treatment for oily skin includes _____ to remove buildup of keratinized cells, then moisturizing with a _____ product for oily skin. It is also important to control the growth of _____ .

13. Describe sensitive skin. _____

_____

_____

14. Products for sensitive skin have fewer sensitizing ingredients, such as _____ and

_____ .

TOPIC 2: Skin Conditions

1. What is hyperpigmentation? _____

2. Freckles, or _____ , are a type of hyperpigmentation, as is _____ , which is hormonally affected and sometimes occurs during pregnancy.

3. Hyperpigmentation is stimulated by any exposure to _____ and may be detected by the esthetician through a _____ .

4. _____ is a condition characterized by small, red, enlarged capillaries, normally on the face and legs. This condition is commonly called _____ .

5. A major cause of dry, dehydrated, and internally injured skin is _____ .

6. One treatment for dark circles around the eyes caused by fatigue is _____ drainage.

7. If you notice an unusual mole or growth on a client's skin, you should _____ _____ .

Word Review

alipidic	distended	pregnancy mask	skin type
couperose	lentigines	secretions	telangiectasia
dehydrated			

CHAPTER 12
Health Screening

Date _____

Rating _____

Text pages: 170–183

Introduction

1. The first step in a facial analysis is _____
   _____ .

2. Hair-removal treatments, such as waxing or laser hair removal, are called _____ .

3. If a drug is contraindicated for a particular treatment, that means it _____
   _____ .
   _____

TOPIC 1: Health Screening Questionnaire

1. Why is it important to find out a client's occupation? _____
   _____
   _____
   _____

2. New clients who have been _____ to you or your salon make great clients.

3. What is the value of the question, "Is this your first facial?" _____
   _____
   _____
   _____

4. Asking clients whether they are under a physician's care will tell you _____
_____ .

5. List four esthetic treatments that are contraindicated for pregnant women.

   a. _____

   b. _____

   c. _____

   d. _____

6. Because birth-control pills cause _____ changes, you should ask clients if they are taking them.

7. Advanced or intensive treatments, such as microcurrent, AHAs and BHAs, and microdermabrasion, require clients to remove _____ if they are worn.

8. Electrical treatments should not be given to:

   a. _____

   b. _____

   c. _____

   d. _____

   e. _____

9. For clients taking antibiotics, many estheticians avoid _____ treatments, such as waxing, AHA treatments, or other kinds of exfoliation.

10. _____ are contraindicated for clients using keratolytic drugs, which work by
_____ . In addition, the following should be avoided with these clients:

   a. _____

   b. _____

   c. _____

   d. _____

   e. _____

   f. _____

   g. _____

11. Skin is said to be more permeable when it is _____
_____ .

12. _____ skin turns red easily during simple esthetic procedures.

13. Waxing and other strong treatments are contraindicated for clients using:

  a. _____ and _____ , also called tretinoin

  b. _____ , a systemic drug that can make skin sensitive long after a client stops taking it

  c. _____ , a systemic drug used to treat autoimmune diseases, such as lupus

14. Why is it important to ask clients to name any products they have obtained from a dermatologist? _____

_____

_____

15. How does Accutane affect the body? _____

_____

_____

16. What should you do if an HIV-positive client comes to you with skin problems, such as herpes, molluscum contagiosum, or unusual rashes? _____

_____

17. Clients with immunodeficiencies should be given treatments that are _____

_____ .

18. Can an esthetician safely treat clients with HIV and AIDS? _____ What about clients with active hepatitis? _____

19. Briefly list precautions you should observe with clients who have the following conditions:

  a. eczema, psoriasis, seborrheic dermatitis: _____

_____

  b. asthma: _____

_____

  c. lupus: _____

_____

_____

  d. herpes simplex: _____

_____

_____

_____

  e. chronic headaches: _____

f. high or low blood pressure: _____

_____

g. chronic blood disorders: _____

_____

20. When clients indicate that they have had acne or frequent blemishes, what follow-up questions should you ask?

a. _____

b. _____

c. _____

21. If a client has had skin cancer, what should you be on the lookout for as you perform treatments? _____

_____

22. A definitive connection has been made between stress and two skin disorders: _____ and _____ .

23. Clients with skin that _____ are more likely to have allergies and to react to irritants.

24. Define the term *allergen*. _____

_____

a. The primary cosmetic allergen is _____ .

b. Another group of common allergens is _____ .

c. _____ , used in acne medication, is a fairly common allergen.

d. A plant extract with anti-inflammatory properties that is also a common allergen is

_____ .

25. Which products are more likely to be allergens, those produced with natural or synthetic ingredients? _____

26. An exfoliant that is overused and causes peeling and redness in clients is considered a(n) _____ rather than an allergen.

27. _____ products cause follicular inflammation that results in acne or pimples.

28. If a client indicates an allergy to aspirin, you should avoid using products containing

_____ .

29. What is a patch test? _____

_____

_____

30. Information about the products a client uses at home tells you about the client's habits as well as the client's:

    a. _____

    b. _____

    c. _____

31. The health-history form includes a medical disclaimer, which ensures that:

    a. _____

_____

    b. _____

32. If a client refuses to fill out the health-history form, you should _____

_____ .

Word Review

allergen	epilation	keratolytic	photoaging
benzoyl peroxide	erythemic skin	medical disclaimer	prednisone
chamomile	hemophilia	neurological	prophylactic
chronic	herpes simplex	patch test	psoriasis
contraindicated	keratinocytes	permeable	rosacea
eczema			

CHAPTER 13
Skin Analysis

Date _____

Rating _____

Text pages: 184–193

Introduction

1. List the three categories into which a skin analysis is divided.

    a. _____

    b. _____

    c. _____

2. Define the term *Fitzpatrick Scale*. _____

    _____

3. Skin with more _____ has greater resistance to sunburn and environmental skin damage.

4. Darker skin types are less likely to suffer from _____ , a decrease in tissue elasticity
   resulting from overexposure to the sun.

5. How is the Fitzpatrick Scale useful to estheticians? _____

    _____

    _____

6. In each of the following spaces, write the Fitzpatrick Scale skin type corresponding to the description.

_____ Mideastern skin types that are rarely sun sensitive

_____ very common skin type; sometimes burns, gradually tans

_____ very fair; red or blonde hair; always burns, never tans

_____ black skin; rarely sun sensitive

_____ fair-skinned; blue, green, or hazel eyes; burns easily

_____ typical Mediterranean Caucasian skin with medium to heavy pigmentation

7. Regardless of coloring, everyone should apply _____ daily.

8. The Fitzpatrick Scale indicates not only sun damage susceptibility but _____ .

9. Hyperpigmentation is more likely to affect skin types _____ , which produce more _____ and are more reactive to stimulation and injuries.

10. PIH, or _____ , is pigmentation resulting from irritation or injury.

TOPIC 1: Skin Analysis Tools

1. Match each of the following skin conditions with its appearance as seen under a Wood's lamp.

_____ oiliness

_____ hypopigmentation

_____ bacteria

_____ normal/combination skin

_____ dehydration/dryness

_____ hyperpigmentation

a. bright or neon yellow

b. overall bluish cast

c. pinkish to orange dots, especially around the nose, chin, and forehead

d. brownish to dark patches where lesions have left marks

e. white patches where there would normally be darker casts

f. bluish to violet to deep purple

2. A mag lamp is useful for observing:

a. _____

b. _____

c. _____

d. _____

3. A _____ shows skin problems and is often used at cosmetic counters to help increase sales of certain skin products.

4. List and briefly describe the stages of a formal analysis procedure.

Step 1: _____
_____

Step 2: _____
_____

Option 1: _____
_____
_____

Option 2: _____
_____

Step 3: _____
_____
_____

5. New clients should be given at least _____ extra minutes for their first appointments.

TOPIC 2: Record Keeping

1. What are the objectives of accurate charting?

a. _____

b. _____
_____

c. _____

d. _____

e. _____

2. In addition to recording which treatments were performed on a client, it is important to note the clients' _____ to these treatments.

TOPIC 3: Closing the Analysis

1. A good skin analysis is based on the three following concepts:

a. _____

b. _____

c. _____

_____

Word Review

charting   Fitzpatrick Scale

CHAPTER 14
Anatomy of a Facial

Date _____

Rating _____

Text pages: 196–227

Introduction

1. All facials begin with _____ and _____ and end with _____ and _____ .

2. Facials increase _____ and _____ circulation, which facilitates the removal of impurities.

TOPIC 1: Products Used in Facials

1. Which kinds of ingredients would be included in a skin-care system targeted to acne skin?
   _____
   _____

2. Which kinds of ingredients would be targeted to mature, dry, environmentally damaged skin?
   _____

3. An accurate analysis of skin type and condition, combined with an understanding of _____ , are the tools an esthetician needs to make informed, appropriate product selections for each client.

4. In each of the following spaces, write the type of product that corresponds to the description. (Please note that terms may be used more than once.)

cleanser	freshener or toner	sunscreen
day cream	mask	washable or foaming
eye makeup remover	night cream	cleanser

_____ provides a smooth base for makeup application

_____ draws and lifts impurities and/or dead cells

_____ dissolves makeup, oil, and surface impurities

_____ is nonalkaline and easy to use

_____ protects the skin from harmful ultraviolet rays

_____ nourishes the skin with treatment ingredients during sleep

_____ softens and moisturizes the delicate eye area

_____ removes traces of makeup and cleanser

_____ tightens and tones the skin

_____ readjusts the skin's pH

_____ acts like soap but lacks the harshness of soap

_____ nongreasy formulas available for contact lens wearers

_____ has nondetergent cleansing ability

TOPIC 2: General Facial Steps

1. List the seven phases of a basic facial.

Phase I: _____

Phase II: _____

Phase III: _____

Phase IV: _____

Phase V: _____

Phase VI: _____

Phase VII: _____

2. What is the purpose of Phase I? _____

_____

a. Describe how to remove eye makeup. _____

_____

_____

_____

_____

b. Lipstick should be removed with _____ .

c. After cleansing and rinsing, how is residue removed? _____

_____

3. What is the purpose of Phase II? _____

_____

a. What is the first step in this process? _____

_____

b. How close should the magnifying light be to the client's skin? _____

c. As you examine the client's face through the magnifying lamp, what else should you be
doing? _____

d. What is the next step? _____

_____

e. A skin analysis normally takes _____ minutes, including any further questions
you may need to ask the client about her skin and health.

4. What is the purpose of Phase III? _____

_____

_____

a. Before you turn the steamer on, you must _____ .

b. When the water in the steamer is boiling, turn on the _____ switch and direct the
steamer toward the client's face at a distance of _____ inches.

c. When cleansing with a brush machine, first dip the brush into _____ and apply it
to the face, beginning at the _____ area. Remove the cleanser with _____ .

d. Describe the disincrustation procedure. _____

_____

_____

_____ • _____

_____

_____

_____

e. Extractions may be performed with _____ or with _____

_____ .

f. Why is it important to avoid force when performing extractions? _____

_____

_____

g. After extractions, what is the next step? _____

_____

_____

5. What is the purpose of Phase IV? _____

_____

a. How is an ampoule used in a facial? _____

_____

6. What is the purpose of Phase V? _____

_____

7. Label each of the massage movements in the following figures.

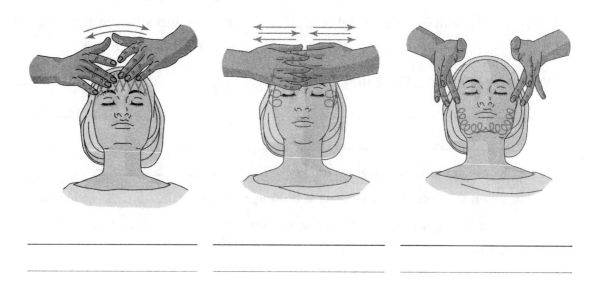

_____   _____   _____

_____   _____   _____

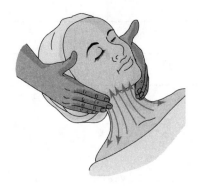

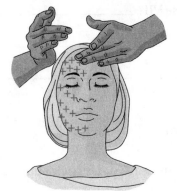

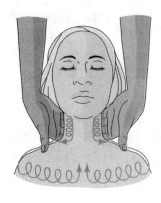

_____   _____   _____

_____   _____   _____

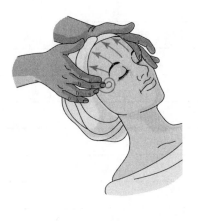

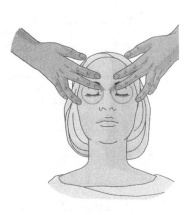

_____   _____   _____

_____   _____   _____

8. What is the purpose of Phase VI? _____

_____

_____

    a. What are the two types of mask usually included in a basic facial? _____

        _____

    b. _____ masks are applied in a soft form and gradually harden on the skin.

    c. About how much mask mixture do you need to prepare? _____

    d. The mask is applied to a _____ thickness, beginning at the _____ , and is

        left on for _____ minutes.

9. What is the purpose of Phase VII? _____

_____

_____

Topic 3: Facial Massage

1. The practice of therapeutic massage dates back about _____ years.

2. Applying massage too _____ or too _____ would counteract most of its beneficial effects.

3. List the benefits of a proper facial massage.

a. _____

b. _____

c. _____

d. _____

e. _____

f. _____

g. _____

h. _____

i. _____

j. _____

k. _____

l. _____

m._____

4. Repetitive motion disorders may be prevented through _____ .

5. Match each of the following massage types with its description.

_____ reflexology

_____ shiatsu

_____ aromatherapy

a. uses essential oils that penetrate the skin during massage

b. uses gentle pressure on the lymphatic system to remove waste materials from the body more quickly

c. combines limb stretching with pressure on acupressure points

_____ acupressure   d. applies gentle but firm pressure to specific points
                                          of the body to release muscle tension and spasm

_____ lymph drainage   e. manipulates areas on the hands and feet

6. Facial massage follows the _____ and _____ phase.

7. In the following chart, describe the five basic massage movements and list the parts of the body
   on which they are used.

Movement	Description	Where Used
effleurage		
petrissage		
friction		
tapotement or percussion		
vibration		

8. In each of the following blanks, write the letter of the corresponding massage movement:

E=effleurage, P=petrissage, F=friction, T=tapotement, V=vibration.

_____ has marked influence on the skin's circulation and glandular activity

_____ stimulates sebum production and expels excess oil

_____ most stimulating movement; should be applied with discretion

_____ warms and softens the skin while relaxing the client

_____ should be used sparingly and never for more than a few seconds in one spot

_____ most important of the five movements

_____ one version is known as the piano movement

_____ rarely used since the advent of small facial vibrators

_____ avoided on skin with nodules or pustules

_____ often used with other types of massage, such as shiatsu

9. Name and describe the three variations of the friction movement.

a. _____

_____

b. _____

_____

c. _____

_____

10. Name the three basic facials and the goals of each.

a. _____

_____

b. _____

_____

c. _____

_____

11. The facial for normal skin does not include Phase _____ .

12. The facial for dry/dehydrated skin offers the three following exfoliation options:

a. _____

b. _____

c. _____

13. For good maintenance, clients should return for facials _____ or _____ .

14. Home-care regimens for different skin types have a few differences and many common elements.

   a. Cleansing and application of freshener and moisturizer are done _____ a day for all skin types.

   b. Cleansing using liquid with beads is recommended for _____ skin.

   c. A gentle scrub is recommended twice weekly for _____ skin.

   d. For all skin types, a _____ is recommended once or twice a week.

   e. Sunblock with an SPF of _____ is part of the daily regimen for all skin types.

15. A minifacial differs from a basic facial in terms of time and content.

   a. Minifacials take _____ minutes to perform.

   b. Minifacials omit _____ .

   c. The most important elements of a minifacial are _____ and _____

      _____ .

Word Review

acupressure	friction	petrissage	tapotement
aromatherapy	lymph drainage	reflexology	vibration
massage	massage	shiatsu	
effleurage			

CHAPTER 15
Men's Facials

Date _____

Rating _____

Text pages: 228–235

Introduction

1. In which ways can male clients be said to be "better" than female clients?

   a. _____

   _____

   b. _____

   c. _____

2. What is a particularly effective way to attract male clients to your salon or spa? _____

   _____

TOPIC 1: Men's Skin-Care Products

1. If the salon's product line does not include a system for men, choose products with the following points in mind:

   a. Men do not like _____ products. Instead, products should be _____

   _____ .

   b. Men prefer _____ routines and _____ products.

   c. _____ cleanser is a good choice because men like the soapiness or foaminess of soap.

   d. _____ are more man-friendly than jars.

e. Men's skin-care regimens should start with only two products: _____ and _____ . A third choice would be _____ . Over time, many clients will add _____ .

f. Male clients should be taught that most movements in the beard and mustache area, such as shaving and washing, should be done in a _____ direction.

g. Many men are conscious of wrinkles around their eyes and can be taught the benefits of _____ .

TOPIC 2: Professional Treatments for Men

1. For cleansing, many men prefer the assertiveness of the _____ .

2. In men's facials, use _____ rather than cotton pads or gauze.

3. If a man shaves just before a facial, the application of _____ may be contraindicated.

4. In which direction should massage movements be directed in the beard area? Why?

_____

_____

_____

_____

5. Define the term *folliculitis*. _____

_____

_____

6. What are the treatment goals for a client with folliculitis?

   a. _____

   b. _____

   c. _____

7. List the steps of a man's deep cleansing facial in sequence.

   a. _____

   b. _____

   _____

   c. _____

   d. _____

e. _____
_____

f. _____

g. _____

h. _____

i. _____

j. _____

k. _____
_____
_____

l. _____

m. _____

n. _____

8. List the commonly waxed areas in male clients.

a. _____

b. _____

c. _____

9. Which two areas of hair growth should estheticians avoid waxing unless they are well trained?

a. _____

b. _____

Discussion Questions

1. How should skin-care products for teenage boys differ from those for middle-aged men?

2. If you were to design the packaging and brochures for a male skin-care line, which colors, graphics, and information would you incorporate?

Word Review

folliculitis

CHAPTER 16
Postconsultation and Home Care

Date _____

Rating _____

Text pages: 236–243

TOPIC 1: Closing Consultation

1. An effective postconsultation achieves the two following basic goals:

   a. _____

   _____

   b. _____

   _____

2. At the end of the facial treatment, before you leave the room, have a brief discussion with the client that includes the following:

   a. _____

   b. _____

   c. _____

   _____

   d. _____

3. While the client is dressing, you can gather the appropriate products and _____

   _____ . Then, review the directions for the products with the client and confirm

   _____ .

TOPIC 2: Developing Long-Term Programs

1. What is the function of a long-term skin-management form? _____
_____
_____
_____

TOPIC 3: Achieving Results

1. If a client refuses to use the home-care products you recommend, what should you do?
_____
_____
_____
_____
_____

TOPIC 4: Follow-Up

1. What is the purpose of a follow-up phone call to a new client 1 or 2 days after the service?
_____
_____
_____

TOPIC 5: Home Care Products

1. On average, about _____ percent of sales in a successful spa or salon are retail sales.

2. One way to overcome a fear of selling is to remember that, unlike department store salespeople, you are serving your customers in a _____ environment.

3. Your goal is not to sell each client your entire product line right away but rather to _____
_____ .

4. Should estheticians guarantee the results of products and treatments? _____
_____
_____

5. To facilitate enrolling your clients into the optimal skin-care system, never sell products by their features but rather by educating clients on the _____ clients will derive from those products.

TOPIC 6: The Home Care Guide

1. What is a home care guide? _____
_____

2. Which elements are essential in any written materials a client sees in the salon, such as home care guides and brochures?

    a. _____

    b. _____

    c. _____

    d. _____
    _____
    _____

    e. _____
    _____
    _____

    f. _____
    _____

3. Which factors necessitate rewriting or updating a home care guide?

    a. _____

    b. _____

    c. _____

    d. _____

4. Why is a home care guide so important? _____
_____
_____

Word Review

home care guide

CHAPTER 17
Disorders and Diseases

Date _____

Rating _____

Text pages: 246–269

TOPIC 1: Common Dermatological Terms

1. How do objective and subjective symptoms differ? _____

   _____

   _____

2. In each of the following blanks, write the letter of the corresponding symptom type: O=objective, S=subjective.

   _____ stinging

   _____ mild pain

   _____ erythema

   _____ itching

   _____ swelling

   _____ rash

3. Any type of skin inflammation is called _____ .

   a. When the skin comes into contact with a sensitizing agent, the result is _____ dermatitis.

   b. Nasal allergies and asthma are examples of _____ dermatitis, which is defined as dermatitis that _____ .

4. Match the following dermatological terms with their definitions.

_____ pathological   a. invasion of body tissue by disease-causing bacteria

_____ hyperkeratosis   b. swelling caused by the body's response to injury or infection

_____ eczema   c. cell buildup

_____ ecchymoses   d. medical term for itching

_____ infection   e. disease causing

_____ purpura   f. redness indicating inflammation

_____ pruritus   g. large bruises

_____ inflammation   h. thickening of the skin due to keratinocytes

_____ keratoses   i. any form of lesion caused by bleeding under the skin

_____ erythema   j. collection of blood under the skin

_____ hematoma   k. advanced, more severe form of dermatitis

5. Benign conditions are not _____ . _____ is the term describing cancerous lesions.

TOPIC 2: Lesions

1. Define the term *lesion*. _____

2. List and describe the three types of lesions.

a. _____

_____

b. _____

_____

c. _____

3. In each of the following blanks, write the letter of the corresponding lesion type: P=primary, S=secondary, V=vascular.

_____ crust

_____ telangiectasia

_____ ecchymosis

_____ ulcer

_____ pustule

_____ keloid

_____ macule

_____ petechia

_____ vesicle

_____ fissure

_____ cherry angioma

_____ tumor

4. Lesion shapes are described as follows:

_____ wavy, shaped like a snake

_____ looks like a target

_____ shaped like a line

_____ ring shaped

_____ shaped like a map

_____ round

5. In the following spaces, write the names of the corresponding macules, or flat lesions.

_____ freckles or lentigines

_____ tiny, pinpoint red spots from trauma

_____ small, red, enlarged capillaries on the face and legs

_____ macules larger than 1 centimeter

_____ freckles resulting from sun damage

_____ red or purple spots that remain from pimples

_____ singular of lentigines

6. Define the term *comedone*. _____

_____

    a. An open comedo, or _____ , has a black top caused by _____ .

    b. A closed comedo has no _____ and appears as a

    _____ .

7. Whiteheads, or _____ , are tiny epidermal _____ just under the skin surface. They

contain _____ but are not always associated with a

_____ .

8. Can milia be removed? _____

_____

9. Identify the following lesions, then find the terms in the following word search puzzle.

_____ solid bump that can be felt, normally larger than 1 centimeter

_____ lesions that have flat surfaces but are raised above the skin

_____ infected papule that has a head with a white or yellow center, which is pus

_____ blister; separation of the epidermis from the upper dermis caused by fluids released by surface blood vessels

_____ deep erosion in which the skin surface is destroyed by infection, poor blood circulation, or cancer

_____ pocket of fluid, infection, or other matter under the skin

_____ mole or birthmark

_____ plaque that is full of fluid

_____ dried body serum, such as pus or blood

_____ very large vesicles

_____ visible lesion that is the result of injury or infection

_____ scar caused by scrapes or scratches

_____ raised lesion, usually red bump; easily felt when touched

_____ flaky skin cell

_____ depression in the skin's surface

_____ very large nodule

N	C	R	Y	U	M	Q	T	J	B	D	Z
O	A	Y	E	L	U	T	S	U	P	C	E
D	T	C	S	F	X	C	L	U	R	M	L
U	H	S	K	T	A	L	L	U	J	W	U
L	I	E	J	R	A	C	S	K	J	I	P
E	S	L	E	E	E	T	U	M	O	R	A
E	X	C	O	R	I	A	T	I	O	N	P
L	D	I	O	U	O	G	W	T	S	L	A
A	N	S	L	R	D	S	G	D	A	L	N
C	Y	E	X	E	I	M	I	Q	T	A	J
S	U	V	E	N	O	C	U	O	Z	N	Y
B	I	Y	R	L	A	E	H	W	N	B	Q

10. What is pus? _____

_____

11. A _____ nodule can be felt and lifted from the skin with two fingers.

12. The medical term for swelling is _____ .

13. How should a blister be handled? _____

_____

14. A scar may be elevated, or _____ . It may also be depressed, or _____ .

15. Describe the disorder known as acne excoriée. _____

_____

_____

16. A _____ nevus is related to blood vessels. A typical example is a _____ ,

which is large, splotchy, and wine colored.

TOPIC 3: Common Conditions and Diseases of the Skin

1. What are skin tags? _____

_____

    a. Another term for skin tags is _____ .

    b. Skin tags are more common in _____ and are often associated with _____ .

    c. They frequently occur on the _____ , _____ , and _____ .

    d. Skin tags are benign and may be removed by a dermatologist by _____ ,

       _____ , or _____

       _____ .

2. Sebaceous hyperplasias are benign lesions that result from _____

_____ .

    a. Hyperplasias must be removed by a _____ or plastic surgeon.

3. The skin condition characterized by redness and bumpiness in the cheeks and upper arms is

   called _____ .

    a. Describe the appearance of this condition. _____

       _____

       _____

b. Who is more likely to have this condition? _____

_____

c. How is this condition treated? _____

_____

_____

4. Define the term *seborrhea*. _____

_____

5. A common form of eczema that primarily affects the oily areas of the face is _____

_____ .

a. This inflammatory disorder is characterized by _____

_____ .

b. It is prevalent in people with _____ , such as AIDS patients.

c. Clients with _____ , _____ , or _____ are also prone to

periodic flare-ups.

d. The best treatment for this condition includes light, fragrance-free products and

_____ cream or lotion. _____ may cause flare-ups.

6. Flaking of the scalp, or _____ , is often caused by seborrheic dermatitis.

7. Rosacea is a common skin condition that usually occurs after age _____ but may begin

earlier.

a. Rosacea is more common in Fitzpatrick skin types _____ , _____ , and _____ .

b. It is characterized by _____

_____ .

c. In mild or early cases, bouts may be triggered by _____ or _____ .

d. More severe cases are characterized by _____ ; very

severe cases are characterized by _____ .

e. In a related condition called _____ , the nose cartilage enlarges.

f. Although no cause has been pinpointed for rosacea, some believe it is caused by small

mites called _____ in the skin. Others believe it is related to a biochemical in the

skin called _____ that is responsible for the formation of new

blood vessels.

g. Rosacea clients should avoid _____ and _____ , as well as such foods as

_____ .

h. Tobacco and caffeine cause _____ , a sudden dilation of blood vessels.

i. Medical treatment of rosacea includes a topical antiyeast medication called

_____ , an oral antibiotic, or _____ .

j. How do dry and oily rosacea differ? _____

_____

_____

_____

k. Place an X by each of the following products, ingredients, and treatments that is recommended for rosacea clients.

_____ grapeseed extract

_____ psolaren

_____ stimulating toner

_____ alcohol-free toner

_____ lightweight broad-spectrum sunscreen

_____ AHA products with very low pH

_____ fragrance-free hydrators

_____ stimulating massage

_____ Lucas sprayer

_____ prolonged steaming

8. An acnelike condition that affects women almost exclusively is _____ .

a. The term *perioral* means _____ .

b. How does this condition appear? _____

_____

_____

c. Among the possible causes of this condition are _____ , because this condition almost always occurs in women, and _____ , because it is treatable with antibiotics.

d. For clients with this condition, an esthetician should recommend a cleanser that is

_____ and moisturizer that is _____

_____ . All _____ should be

temporarily discontinued in that area.

9. Poison ivy is an example of _____ .

10. Everyone who comes in skin contact with a highly acidic material develops _____

dermatitis.

11. One difference between ACD and ICD is that _____

_____ .

12. _____ , or hives, is an allergic reaction. The hives result from edema and the release of

_____ .

13. If a client reacts to a salon treatment with hives, you should _____

_____ .

TOPIC 4: Common Allergens in the Skin-Care Business

1. The most common allergen in skin-care products is _____ .

2. Another common cosmetic allergen is _____ .

3. Match the following terms with their definitions.

_____ pityriasis rosea   a. genetic skin condition prevalent in people with asthma, airborne nasal allergies, and overreactive immune systems

_____ overproliferation   b. common condition characterized by red patches of skin that may be round or oval

_____ atopic dermatitis   c. disease associated with the rate of cell turnover or cell renewal

_____ dermatosis papulosa nigra   d. first red patch that appears in a common skin condition

_____ herald patch   e. skin cells replicating too quickly

_____ proliferative disease   f. black or brown lesions that look like moles and occur in black skin

4. Psoriasis is a hereditary, _____ disease.

     a. It is prevalent in people with _____ diseases.

     b. Describe the visible symptoms of psoriasis. _____

_____

_____

     c. How is psoriasis treated? _____

_____

_____

TOPIC 5: Contagious Diseases

1. Unscramble the following terms and use them to fill in the blanks in the following sentences.

feincootutausi	VSH 2	etian pirroocs
calbretai vinjicottiscun	goitepmi	neita spied
dolc resso	slummcoul mogaitoncsu	inaet crevoorlis
sheerp mixselp rusiv 1	nipoystopor	straw
mahun vapplomilausir	antie	

   a. The medical term for athlete's foot is _____ .

   b. Warts are caused by the _____ .

   c. A contagious bacterial skin infection that often occurs in young children is

      _____ .

   d. _____ are skin infections caused by fungi.

   e. Genital herpes is caused by _____ .

   f. _____ lesions can spread to other areas on the same person.

   g. A contagious viral infection that appears as clusters of small, flesh-colored papules is

      _____ .

   h. In some people, a yeast called _____ infects the skin and affects the skin's ability to produce melanin.

   i. Estheticians can perform exfoliation on clients with _____ only if those clients are pretreated with an antiviral drug prescribed by a physician.

   j. The fungal infection commonly known as ringworm is _____ .

   k. HSV 1 causes _____ and is commonly spread by kissing.

   l. _____ are caused by a virus and treated with cryosurgery and OTC products containing salicylic acid.

   m. A client with _____ should not wear eye makeup as long as the infection is present.

   n. White splotches of hypopigmentation are typical of the yeast infection called

      _____ .

TOPIC 6: Other Diseases of the Skin

1. Write descriptions of the following diseases and their standard medical treatment(s) (if any) in the spaces provided.

Disease	Description	Treatment
folliculitis		
hypopigmentation		
dyschromia		
erysipelas		
shingles		
albinism		
hyperpigmentation		
melasma		

(continued)

Disease	Description	Treatment
vitiligo		
cellulitis		

2. The cause of shingles is the _____ virus, which also causes _____ .

3. Shingles is most common in older people or those with _____ .

4. Shaving in the direction of hair growth and not too close to the skin can prevent a condition called _____ . OTC preparations for ingrown hairs contain _____ , which breaks up the impaction and kills bacteria.

5. Mottling, solar lentigines, and poikiloderma of Civatte are all types of _____ .

6. Acne or eczema can result in PIH, or _____ .

7. Because _____ skin types are more susceptible to hyperpigmentation, estheticians should be particularly careful when performing extraction and exfoliation.

8. Hydroquinone interferes with the production of _____ .

9. Topical ingredients that estheticians can use to help suppress melanin production and lighten hyperpigmentation include:

a. _____

b. _____

c. _____

d. _____

e. _____

f. _____

g. _____

TOPIC 7: Autoimmune Diseases

1. People with AIDS and similar diseases are said to be _____ or

_____ or to have _____ .

2. What is an autoimmune disease? _____

_____

_____

3. AIDS is caused by the _____ , or HIV.

4. An autoimmune disease that features a butterfly-shaped rash on the face is _____

_____ . It is treated with prescription _____ .

5. A form of lupus that primarily affects the skin is DLE, or _____ .

     a. Describe the appearance of DLE. _____

       _____

       _____

     b. With a physician's approval, an esthetician can treat the skin of a lupus patient using

       products designed for _____ .

     c. The most important product for clients with lupus is a _____

       _____ for daily use.

6. What is dermatomyositis? _____

_____

7. _____ is an autoimmune disease that makes the skin very tight and thick.

Discussion Questions

1. Why is it important that estheticians understand medical terminology?

2. Explain why it is important—to you and your clients—that you be able to recognize various skin disorders.

3. Create a dialogue in which you let a client know that you think the client has a potentially serious skin disease that should be examined by a physician.

Word Review

acne excoriée	actinic lentigines	atopic dermatitis	cellulitis

acquired immunodefi-
   ciency syndrome
   (AIDS)
	albinism
	
	allergic contact der-
	   matitis (ACD)
		autoinfectious
		
		bacterial conjunctivitis
		benign
			chickenpox
			
			closed comedo
			cold sores

acrochordons	annular	bullae	comedones

contact dermatitis

crust

cyst

dandruff

demodex

dermatitis

dermatomyositis

dermatosis papulosa
   nigra

dyschromia

ecchymoses

erosion

erysipelas

erythema

excoriation

flares of rosacea

geographic

hematoma

herald patch

herpes simplex virus 1
   (HSV 1)

herpes simplex virus 2
   (HSV 2)

herpes zoster

human immunodefi-
   ciency virus (HIV)

human papillo-
   mavirus (HPV)

hydroquinone

hyperkeratosis

hyperpigmented
   macules

hypopigmentation

hypotrophic

impetigo

infection

inflammation

irritant contact
   dermatitis (ICD)

keratoses

keratosis pilaris

lentigo

lesion

linear

macule

malignant

melasma

metronidazole

milia

molluscum contagio-
   sum

nevus

objective symptoms

open comedo

overproliferation

papule

patches

pathological

perioral dermatitis

petechiae

pityosporon

pityriasis rosea

port-wine stain

proliferative diseases

pruritus

purpura

pus

pustule

rhinophyma

rounded

scars

sclerodema

seborrhea

seborrheic dermatitis

sepiginous

shingles

skin tags

solar lentigines

subjective symptoms

target

tinea

tinea corporis

tinea pedis

tinea versicolor

ulcer

vascular

vascular growth factor
   (VGF)

vascular macules

vasodilation

vitiligo

warts

CHAPTER 18
Pharmacology

Date _____

Rating _____

Text pages: 270–281

Introduction

1. Define the term *pharmacology*. _____

_____

2. According to the FDA, drugs are intended to _____

_____ .

TOPIC 1: Over-the-Counter and Prescription Drugs

1. What is the difference between over-the-counter (OTC) and prescription drugs? _____

_____

_____

2. The federal agency responsible for approving all new drugs is the _____

_____ .

3. After approval, most drugs are offered as prescription drugs initially. Why is it important that these drugs be restricted through prescription before they are made available over the counter?

_____

_____

_____

_____

4. Which three types of OTC drugs do estheticians use and sell in the United States?

    a. _____

    b. _____

    c. _____

5. A sunscreen is marketed as _____ if it screens out a large portion of the light spectrum.

6. Sunscreens work by _____ or _____ ultraviolet rays.

7. Explain how physical or particulate sunscreens work. _____

_____

_____

_____

8. Only the two following reflecting ingredients are approved for sunscreen:

    a. _____

    b. _____

9. Why is the term *sunblock* no longer used? _____

_____

_____

10. In the micronization process, the pigments in particulate sunscreens are _____ _____ so that they are basically invisible on most skin colors.

11. How do chemical sunscreens differ from physical sunscreens? _____

_____

_____

12. Name three active ingredients often combined in sunscreen to enhance the spectrum of light absorbed, and list their functions in the product.

    a. _____

    b. _____

    c. _____

13. Name two disadvantages and one advantage of absorbing sunscreens.

    a. disadvantages: _____

                     _____

    b. advantage: _____

14. For oily and combination skin, sunscreens in the form of ultralight lotions and fluids that are not _____ are the best choice.

15. Describe the test a sunscreen must pass to be called water resistant. _____

_____

16. The labels on OTC drugs, including sunscreens, must list _____ first.

17. In Europe, sunscreens are considered _____ , so you must check the labels on any European sunscreens you use or sell.

18. Which bacteria causes acne vulgaris? _____

19. List the four ingredients approved for OTC acne treatments.

   a. _____

   b. _____

   c. _____

   d. _____

20. The topical drugs in OTC acne treatments kill the bacteria that cause acne vulgaris or _____

_____ .

21. _____ bacteria thrive in the absence of oxygen and cannot live in the presence of oxygen.

22. Name and briefly describe two factors that cause acne.

   a. _____

   _____

   b. _____

   _____

23. What is the most widely used OTC acne drug, and what are the two ways in which it is effective against acne? _____

_____

_____

24. Before using benzoyl peroxide on a client, you should _____ .

25. What is the most effective way to use benzoyl peroxide? _____

_____

_____

26. Describe the other ingredients used in OTC acne treatments.

    a. salicylic acid: _____

    _____

    b. sulfur: _____

    _____

    c. sulfur-resorcinol: _____

    _____

    _____

27. Granular scrubs for acne skin use _____ to "bump off" dead cells and contain a high concentration of _____ , which help remove excess sebum.

28. _____ that are dabbed directly on acne lesions are generally reserved for clients with occasional pimples, while _____ are used on clients with chronic acne flares.

29. Masks for acne generally use a _____ base as well as active OTC ingredients, usually _____ or _____ .

30. Moisturizers for acne skin may contain _____ .

TOPIC 2: Skin-Lightening Products

1. What is hydroquinone, and how does it work? _____

    _____

    _____

2. Hydroquinone is often combined in gel formulations with _____ , an AHA.

3. Hydroquinone is used in concentrations up to _____ percent in OTC products and up to _____ percent in prescription products.

4. One drawback to hydroquinone is that it causes _____ .

5. Ingredients that have similar lightening effects as hydroquinone but are not approved as OTC drugs are known as _____ . They include:

    a. _____

    b. _____

    c. _____

    d. _____

    e. _____

    f. _____

6. Any skin-lightening regimen must include daily use of a _____

_____ .

7. Hydroquinone products should not be left in _____ .

TOPIC 3: Corticosteroids

1. Hormones that help relieve inflammation, itching, and redness are called _____ .

2. Hydrocortisone in up to 1 percent concentration in OTC products is used to treat minor rashes and redness from _____ , _____ , and _____ .

3. Hydrocortisone should never be used on a daily basis for longer than _____ at a time without a physician's approval. Overuse can cause the skin to become _____ .

TOPIC 4: Prescription Steroids

1. Many steroids are prescribed to treat the _____ rather than the causes of skin diseases.

2. Temovate, Diprolene, Elocon, and Topicort are all prescription _____ .

3. You should avoid overly stimulating treatments for clients using _____ , a widely prescribed oral steroid.

TOPIC 5: Allergic Reactions, Hives, and Redness

1. Define the term *antihistamine*. _____

_____

TOPIC 6: Retinoids

1. Retinoids are _____ .

2. Retin-A is the retinoid drug _____ . This drug has _____ properties, which means it loosens comedones.

3. Tretinoin was originally designed as a _____ and is now also approved by the FDA for the treatment of _____ .

4. Clients using Retin-A or Renova must avoid the following products:

a. _____

b. _____

c. _____

d. _____

e. _____

5. These clients should also avoid treatments such as _____ and _____ .

6. Tretinoin users should apply _____ daily to protect their skin and should use tretinoin at night because _____ .

7. A salon facial for a client using tretinoin should consist of:

a. _____

b. _____

c. _____

d. _____

e. _____

8. Many clients today use _____ instead of tretinoin to avoid some of the side effects of tretinoin.

9. Match each of the following drugs with its description.

_____ sulfacetamide   a. isotretinoin; used to treat cystic acne

_____ tazarotene   b. retinoid with actions and side effects similar to tretinoin

_____ adapalene   c. topical drug prescribed for rosacea; oily, acnelike flares; and acne vulgaris

_____ Accutane   d. topical antibiotic sometimes combined with benzoyl peroxide to treat acne

_____ metronidazole   e. antiviral medication used to treat herpes simplex

_____ acyclovir   f. prescription drug most commonly used to treat rosacea

_____ erythromycin   g. retinoid originally used for psoriasis but now used to treat acne

10. Adapalene is also known as _____ .

11. _____ is the only drug that causes sebaceous glands to shrink and normalize.

12. What are two important medical side effects of isotretinoin?

    a. _____

    b. _____

13. What are the side effects of Accutane that affect the skin? _____

_____

14. Clients taking Accutane should stop using _____ products, including several months after they have stopped taking the drug.

15. Describe the following products clients taking Accutane should use.

    cleanser   _____

    toner   _____

    moisturizer   _____

    sunscreen   _____

    mask   _____

TOPIC 7: Drugs for the Treatment of Rosacea

1. MetroGel, Metrolotion, Metrocream, and Noritate are all commercial names for the prescription drug _____ .

2. A patient taking any of these drugs should avoid:

    a. _____

    b. _____

    c. _____

    d. _____

    e. _____

3. Rosacea skin can be calmed by products with such soothing agents as _____ or

_____ .

TOPIC 8: Antibiotics

1. Drugs that kill bacteria are called _____ .

2. Why are prescriptions required for the use of antibiotics? _____

_____

3. Tetracycline, erythromycin, and doxycycline are all _____ prescribed for bacterial skin infections.

4. Warts, cold sores, shingles, and genital herpes are treated with _____ drugs.

Word Review

Accutane	broad spectrum	pharmacology	resorcinol
adapalene	comedolytic	prescription drugs	salicylic acid
anaerobic	corticosteroids	Propionibacterium	sulfacetamide
antibiotics	over-the-counter	acnes	sulfur
antihistamine	(OTC) drugs	Renova	tazarotene

CHAPTER 19

Product Chemistry

Date _____

Rating _____

Text pages: 282–301

Introduction

1. Many of the functions of the skin are actually _____ reactions.

2. Define the term *biochemistry*. _____

_____

3. Which of the following statements are true?

_____ Natural ingredients are chemical free.

_____ All chemicals cause irritation or allergic reactions.

_____ Natural extracts and substances are made of chemicals.

_____ More than two-thirds of all drugs are derived from plants.

_____ Some chemicals have positive effects on the skin.

_____ All cosmetics and skin-care products are chemicals.

4. What is an applied science? _____

_____

TOPIC 1: Basic Chemistry

1. Chemical changes, bodily functions, and the effects of skin-care products are all based on the chemical reactions that take place when chemicals exchange _____ .

2. Define the following terms:

element _____

_____

compound _____

atom _____

nucleus _____

protons _____

neutrons _____

electrons _____

ionic bond _____

3. Oxygen and iron are examples of _____ . Iron oxide, or rust, is a _____ .

4. How do the atoms of different elements differ? _____

_____

5. In its most basic state, an atom has the same number of _____ and _____ .

6. Electrons travel in orbits called _____ .

7. How one atom reacts with another is determined by _____

_____ .

8. Explain this important principle: "All atoms have a physical need to have a full outer energy level." _____

_____

_____

_____

9. Atoms are called ions when they _____ .

10. When atoms form an ionic or covalent bond, they create a _____ .

11. In a covalent bond, two atoms _____ .

12. How is a free radical formed? _____

_____

_____

_____

13. A good source of electrons that are easy for free radicals to steal is the _____ in the skin.

14. Once the oxygen atoms have stolen electrons, what is the result? _____

_____

_____

TOPIC 2: Cosmetic Ingredients

1. How does the FDA define the term *cosmetics*? _____

_____

_____

2. Name and describe the two basic types of cosmetic ingredients.

    a. _____

    _____

    b. _____

3. What other terms are used to refer to performance ingredients?

    a. _____

    b. _____

    c. _____

4. What is the action of each of the following ingredients on the skin?

    a. alphahydroxy acids   _____

    b. glycerin   _____

    c. lipids   _____

5. Products intended to improve the skin's health and appearance may be classified as

    _____ .

6. What is the FDA's role in the approval or regulation of skin-care products and cosmetics?

_____

_____

_____

7. According to the FDA, only claims related to _____ can be made for cosmetics.

8. FDA regulations stipulate that product ingredients must be listed in _____ order, from the ingredient with the _____ concentration to that with the _____ concentration.

9. The most commonly used cosmetic ingredient is _____ .

10. What are the functions of water in cosmetics?

    a. as a vehicle: _____

    b. as a performance ingredient: _____

11. Almost all skin-care products are a mixture of _____ and_____ .

12. List and define the two types of emulsions used in skin care products.

    a. _____

    b. _____

13. Anhydrous products are generally designed for _____ skin. They contain no _____ and include oil serums and _____ -based products.

14. Emollients are almost always _____ agents.

15. What are the functions of emollients in skin-care products?

    a. as vehicles: _____

    b. as performance ingredients: _____

    _____

16. Emollients lie on the skin and prevent _____ by trapping water, a process called _____ .

17. Mineral oil and petrolatum are emollients that come from _____ in the earth.

18. The key ingredient in classic cold cream and baby oil is _____ .

19. Mineral oil and petrolatum are safe and effective emollients. Name six advantages of using them in cosmetic formulations.

    a. _____

    b. _____

    c. _____

    d. _____

    e. _____

    f. _____

20. What does it mean to say that an ingredient is biologically inert? _____

_____

21. Why do mineral oil and petrolatum not need preservatives? _____

_____

22. Plant oils are made of _____ components.

23. Plant oils are very similar to human _____ , which is beneficial for skin that produces too little.

24. Identify the following emollients by type: FA=fatty acid, FALC=fatty alcohol, S=silicone, FE=fatty ester.

_____ fatty acid that has been exposed to hydrogen

_____ has lost favor, because plant-derived ingredients are more popular

_____ examples are tridecyl stearate, octyl palmitate, and isopropyl palmitate

_____ lubricant ingredient derived from plant oils or animal fats

_____ keeps moisture trapped in skin but allows oxygen in and out of the follicles

_____ emollient produced from fatty acids and alcohols

_____ mineral-based substance used as lightweight emollient and vehicle

_____ names almost always end in -ate

_____ stearyl alcohol and cetyl alcohol are examples

25. List the uses and benefits of these emollients:

a. fatty esters: _____

b. fatty acids: _____

_____

c. fatty alcohols: _____

_____

d. silicones: _____

_____

26. Define the term *comedogenicity*. _____

_____

_____

27. The most comedogenic cosmetic ingredient is _____ .

28. The only food source for the bacteria that cause acne vulgaris is _____ .

29. The comedogenicity of a product is determined in part by the concentration of _____

_____ .

30. When ingredients are tested alone, without combining them with other ingredients, they are

in their _____ form.

31. Heavier emollients are helpful for which types of skin? _____ For which types

of skin are these emollients *not* intended? _____

32. If you are not sure a product has been tested for comedogenicity, it would be wise to _____

_____

_____ .

33. Identify which of the following ingredients are highly comedogenic, moderately comedogenic,

mildly comedogenic, and noncomedogenic by writing HC, MODC, MC, or NC in the appro-

priate spaces.

_____ grapeseed oil

_____ olive oil

_____ safflower oil

_____ octyl palmitate

_____ allantoin

_____ petrolatum

_____ sesame oil

_____ mineral oil

_____ lanolin

_____ jojoba oil

_____ tocopherol

_____ squalene

_____ lanolic acid

_____ avocado oil

_____ lauric acid

_____ sodium hyaluronate

34. Fill in the blanks in the following sentences with one of the following terms. (Please note that not all terms are used.)

become slippery	foam	silicone
detergent	irritancy	spreadability
emollient	mineral	surface tension
fat	sebum	surfactants

a. Silicones are _____ -based substances used as lightweight emollients and vehicles.

b. Cyclomethicone, dimethicone, and phenyl trimethicone are noncomedogenic _____ -based ingredients with very low _____ potential.

c. _____ are ingredients that reduce the surface tension between the skin and the product. They are used to improve the _____ of skin-care and cosmetic products.

d. The main surfactant used in skin-care products is _____ .

e. Detergents in cleansing products have two effects: they reduce the _____ of dirt and oils, which helps lift them off the skin, and they also cause cleansers to _____ .

f. Detergents that are too strong or too concentrated damage the lipid barrier function by removing too much _____ .

35. Identify the following types of detergent or cleanser:

_____ most common detergent in skin cleansers; used frequently in shampoo

_____ less aggressive and irritating detergent used in rinse-off cleansers for oily and combination skins

_____ cleansers with low concentrations of detergent that do not foam very much; used on dry skin

_____ newer cleansing agent that is much milder than sulfates

36. Emulsifiers are another type of _____ . What is their function in products? _____

_____

37. A product that must be shaken before it is used, to mix it, is a _____ .

38. Substances in a product that are compatible with oil are called _____ , and those that are mixable with water are called _____ . When an emulsifier is added to the oil and water phases, an _____ forms.

39. _____ are nonfoaming, usually oil-in-water emulsions that are excellent for removing makeup. They are also called _____ .

40. A carbomer is a vehicle ingredient used to _____ creams and is often used in gel products.

41. What is the pH scale, and why is pH important to the esthetician? _____

   _____

   _____

42. On the following pH scale, identify where each of the following substances falls:

sodium bicarbonate	lye	depilatories
peroxide	pure water	skin
soap	lemon juice	

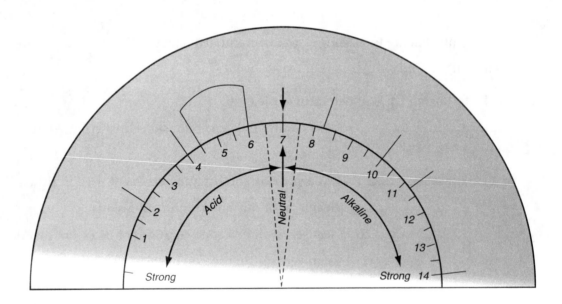

43. Which pH range is considered acidic? _____ Which range is considered alkaline?

   _____

44. The pH scale is a _____ scale.

    a. A pH of 6 is 10 times more acidic than a pH of _____ .

    b. A pH of 12 is 100 times more alkaline than a pH of _____ .

45. Define the term acid mantle and explain its function. _____

_____

_____

46. What is the pH of the acid mantle? _____

47. _____ may result if the skin is exposed to low or high pH. To keep pHs at safe levels, pH adjusters or _____ are often added to skin-care products.

48. _____ fragrances are used to cover any unpleasant smells or ingredients in skin-care products.

49. What are aromatherapy or essential oils? _____

_____

50. The international term for fragrance is _____ .

51. Which two functions do preservatives perform in cosmetic products?

    a. _____

    _____

    b. _____

52. Antioxidants, which inhibit _____ , serve the two following general functions in products:

    a. _____

    b. _____

53. Oxidation may be defined as _____ , a process that damages the _____ of cells.

    a. As soon as a product is opened and exposed to air, it begins to _____ .

    b. _____ are added to products to prevent this process.

    c. Define the term *microencapsulation*. _____

    _____

    d. Is microencapsulation used on antioxidants that keep products fresh? _____

    _____

54. Name and describe the two types of color ingredients.

a. _____

_____

_____

b. _____

_____

_____

55. What are delivery systems? _____

_____

56. What are the three ways in which delivery systems are used?

a. _____

b. _____

c. _____

57. Name and briefly describe two commonly used delivery systems.

a. _____

_____

b. _____

_____

58. What are the benefits of improving the moisture level of the epidermis?

a. _____

b. _____

c. _____

d. _____

59. The two basic treatments for dry and dehydrated skin involve the use of occlusive and hydrating products.

a. What do occlusive agents do? _____

_____

b. What do hydrators do? _____

_____

c. Hydrators are also called _____ or _____ .

d. Most moisturizing products are combinations of _____ and _____ .

e. Areas such as the _____ and _____ require more emollients than other areas of the face.

60. The natural barrier function is made primarily of lipids.

    a. What are the two functions of these lipids? _____

    _____

    b. In addition to moisturizing, how do occlusive agents help restore the skin's barrier function? _____

    _____

    c. For postlaser resurfacing patients, the best occlusive product to protect against moisture loss is _____ .

61. In the following spaces below, write A next to products that should be avoided by clients with sensitive skin and S for soothing products that help these clients.

    _____ fragrance ingredients

    _____ chamomile

    _____ color agents

    _____ highly acidic or alkaline products

    _____ stimulants

    _____ azulene

    _____ most exfoliants

    _____ green tea extract

    _____ stearyl glycyrrhetinate

62. _____ is the removal of dead corneum cells.

63. How do mechanical exfoliating ingredients work on the skin? _____

_____

    a. Name some commonly used mechanical exfoliators.

    _____

    _____

    _____

    _____

64. How do chemical exfoliating ingredients work? _____

_____

    a. What are the two most commonly used categories of chemical exfoliators?

    _____

    _____

b. List some examples.

_____

_____

_____

_____

_____

_____

65. What are proteolytic enzymes? Name three examples. _____

_____

66. What are the two general categories of masks, and what is their main difference?

a. _____

b. _____

67. Name the three basic functions of setting masks.

a. _____

b. _____

c. _____

68. Setting masks generally use _____ as their base.

69. Nonsetting masks are intended mostly for _____ and sensitive skins. Their main functions are to _____ and _____ .

Word Review

acid mantle	carbomer	element	hydrophilic agents
acids	certified colors	emollients	ionic bond
alkalines	coconut oil	emulsifiers	kaolin
anhydrous	comedogenic	emulsion	lakes
applied science	comedogenicity	energy levels	liposomes
aromatherapy oils	compound	fatty alcohols	microencapsulation
atom	cosmeceuticals	fatty esters	microsponge
bentonite	cosmetics	free radicals	neat
biochemistry	delivery systems	functional ingredients	neutrons
biologically inert	detergent	humectants	noncertified colors
buffering agents	diatomaceous earth	hydrators	noncomedogenic

nonsetting masks

nucleus

occlusion

occlusive agents

oil-in-water (O/W)
    emulsions

oil soluble

opacifiers

oxidation

palm oil

parfum

performance
    ingredients

protons

setting masks

silicones

surfactants

water-in-oil (W/O)
    emulsions

water soluble

CHAPTER 20
Advanced Ingredient Technology

Date _____

Rating _____

Text pages: 302–307

TOPIC 1: Food and Drug Regulations

1. The FDA views cosmetics in accordance with the _____ of 1938.

2. According to the FDA, how do drugs differ from cosmetics? _____

_____

_____

_____

3. Estheticians focus on improving the skin's appearance. They cannot claim that a product or treatment can affect the _____ .

TOPIC 2: Serums

1. _____ , _____ , and _____ are user-friendly versions of ampoules that are available retail.

2. Serums are designed as a corrective treatment to be used for _____ or more, while professional _____ are intended for immediate, one-time use.

3. Today's serums may be as potent as more traditional ampoules because of _____

_____ .

4. Estheticians can educate their clients on the benefits of serums by:

a. _____

_____

b. _____

c. _____

TOPIC 3: Delivery Systems

1. Liposomes transfer ingredients to the skin by _____ .

2. Liposomes are often given names such as "microspheres of moisture" in advertising and efficacy claims to avoid _____ among users.

3. What are nanosomes? _____

_____

4. Define the term polymers. _____

_____

_____

5. How were the uses of polymers discovered and by whom? _____

_____

_____

_____

6. How are polymers used in products for oily skin? _____

_____

7. Why is polymer technology of such great importance to the skin-care industry? _____

_____

TOPIC 4: Improving Cell Metabolism

1. Name four high-tech antioxidants that stimulate metabolic processes and explain briefly how they help the skin.

a. _____

_____

_____

_____

b. _____

_____

c. _____

_____

d. _____

_____

_____

TOPIC 5: Nature versus Biotechnology

1. One drawback of natural ingredients is that they may cause _____ in sensitive clients.

2. An ingredient in cosmetic formulations that was originally derived from roosters' combs is

_____ .

3. How can estheticians make informed choices between natural and bioengineered cosmetics?

_____

4. In which ways are biotechnical ingredients sometimes improvements over the natural ingredients they emulate? _____

_____

_____

Word Review

beta-glucans	nanosomes	polymers	tissue respiratory
coenzyme Q10	polyglucans	serums	factor (TRF)
glycoproteins			

CHAPTER 21
Aging Skin: Morphology and Treatment

Date _____

Rating _____

Text pages: 310–339

TOPIC 1: Intrinsic Aging

1. _____ aging occurs because of heredity, genetic factors, and general physiology. _____ aging factors are controllable and not genetically predetermined.

2. Skin coloring, sensitivity, and oiliness or dryness are among many characteristics determined by our _____ .

3. Wrinkles, or _____ , are caused mostly by the repetition of facial expressions or by cumulative _____ .

4. Smile lines and crow's feet are types of _____ , which may be defined as _____ _____ _____ .

5. The muscles of the face are attached to the _____ .

6. _____ folds go from the corners of the nose to the mouth.

7. The lines around smokers' mouths are caused by repetitive facial movements and by _____ _____ .

8. Gravity pulls down on the body and skin, causing a lack of skin elasticity, or _____ .

9. In each of the following spaces, write the appropriate age range: 20s, 30s, 40s, MP (menopause), 50s, or 60+.

_____ production of estrogen slows

_____ elastosis is much more apparent; jowls may begin to form

_____ expression lines begin to show; upper eyebrow skin begins to lose elasticity

_____ cumulative damage from years of sun exposure becomes more visible

_____ bones in the skull may appear more obvious because of loss of subcutaneous fat

_____ skin begins to droop because of gravity, continued loss of collagen

_____ cartilage of nose and ears expands due to gravity

_____ acne flares may occur, caused by hormonal shifts

_____ bones in the body and face begin to shrink

10. In the midtwenties, collagen in the skin begins to diminish at the rate of _____ percent per year.

11. The loss of skin elasticity in the upper eyelid is called _____ .

12. Fill in the following blanks with the correct terms from the following list. (Please note that not all terms are used.)

acne	estrogen	rosacea
androgen	lipid	sebum
barrier function	melanocytes	testosterone
collagen	progesterone	

a. At menopause, women begin to produce less _____ . As a result, the production and repair of _____ in the skin decreases.

b. Changing hormone levels affect _____ production between the cells in the skin's barrier.

c. The production of _____ diminishes, causing superficial dehydration.

d. Some menopausal women experience a flare in _____ . As estrogen levels drop, another female hormone, _____ , prompts the sebaceous glands to produce more sebum.

13. List the effects of estrogen on the skin.

    a. _____

    b. _____

    c. _____

    d. _____

    e. _____

    f. _____

14. In a person's fifties, the face goes through certain _____ changes, which are changes in shape and form.

15. Most of the physiological changes of the skin occur in the _____ as the rate of collagen and _____ replacement decreases.

16. Many epidermal changes can be treated by the esthetician.

    a. The rate of epidermal renewal, normally about _____ days, slows with aging.

    b. This slowdown causes cells to _____ on the surface and the skin to look dull.

    c. Gaps in the intercellular lipid structure lead to easier penetration by _____ _____ .

    d. Older skin becomes more sensitive because of _____ _____ .

    e. These epidermal changes are most effectively treated with _____ .

TOPIC 2: Extrinsic Aging

1. Many experts believe that extrinsic factors may account for _____ percent of the visible signs of skin aging.

2. Repeated exposure to the sun alters and damages the following skin structures:

    a. _____

    b. _____

    c. _____

    d. _____

    e. _____

    f. _____

3. Unscramble the following words and use them to identify the following terms:

hoopgantig	stormeeann	thomialeedrisso
nacciti agamed		

_____ general skin damage associated with sun exposure

_____ unit of measurement for the light spectrum

_____ technical term for sun-induced aging symptoms

_____ common term for aging symptoms related to sun exposure

4. How do UVA and UVB rays differ? _____

_____

_____

5. What causes tanning? _____

_____

_____

6. Match the following terms with their definitions or descriptions:

_____ free radicals   a. one of the most reactive elements

_____ hydroxy radicals   b. one of the best sources of electrons

_____ subclinical inflammation   c. wild molecules or atoms that have lost electrons and are unstable

_____ lipid peroxides   d. inflammation not visible to the eye

_____ iron   e. another term for unstable oxygen atom, or free radical

_____ superoxide   f. free radicals formed when cell membrane is damaged

_____ cell membrane   g. most dangerous free radicals

7. Sun exposure causes stable _____ molecules to split, producing one stable and one unstable atom. The unstable atom is called a _____ .

8. How do free radicals damage the cell membrane? _____

_____

_____

_____

9. Peroxides react with the iron in blood hemoglobin to form _____ .

10. At the cellular level, the real cause of skin aging is damage to the _____ in future cells produced through cell division.

11. Define the term *crosslinking*. _____

_____

_____

12. Free radicals can cause _____ inflammation, whose symptoms are not visible.

13. When skin cells are inflamed, white blood cells signal them to make _____ such as elastase and collagenase.

14. The conditions surrounding any inflammation support _____ activity that damages the skin.

15. One of the effects of short-term sun damage is _____ of the epidermis by repelling macrophages.

16. Explain briefly how years of sun damage can lead to skin cancer. _____

_____

_____

_____

17. Sunburn is a(n) _____ response to sun exposure.

18. The most immediate sign of inflammation from sun damage is redness, or _____ . It is caused by _____ .

19. How should an esthetician treat a client with sunburned skin? _____

_____

20. What advice can you offer a sunburned client?

a. _____

b. _____

c. _____

d. _____

e. _____

f. _____

21. Match the following terms with their definitions:

_____ solar urticaria
a. precancerous lesions caused by sun damage

_____ seborrheic keratosis
b. easy bruising of the skin

_____ senile purpura
c. surface growth or thickening of epidermal cells

_____ solar lentigines
d. phototoxic reaction in a person taking a drug such as tetracycline or sulfur

_____ polymorphous light eruption
e. hives associated with sun exposure

_____ mottling
f. freckles caused by sun exposure

_____ actinic keratoses
g. form of speckled hyperpigmentation

22. Match the following terms with their definitions:

_____ solar elastosis
a. tiny dilated blood vessels in the skin

_____ crisscross wrinkling
b. roughness in the feel of the skin associated with sun damage

_____ poikiloderma of Cevattes
c. severe sagging in sun-damaged skin

_____ tactile roughness
d. solar comedones

_____ telangiectasias
e. dark splotches of hyperpigmentation; very intense solar lentigines

_____ Favre-Racouchot
f. telangiectasia and hyperpigmentation in a horseshoe pattern on the neck

_____ liver spots
g. wrinkling in crossed patterns, typical in sun-damaged skin

23. _____ may occur when a client is taking photoreactive drugs and appears as a rash in the central areas of the face.

24. Red, swollen, itching, or burning lesions that appear after sun exposure may be symptoms of _____ .

25. List and briefly describe the symptoms of sun damage.

a. _____

_____

b. _____

c. _____

_____

d. _____

e. _____

f. _____

_____

g. _____

h. _____

i. _____

j. _____

_____

k. _____

_____

l. _____

26. What causes mottling and solar lentigines? _____

_____

27. At which stage in life does most sun damage occur? _____

28. How are telangiectasias medically treated? How are they treated by estheticians?

a. medical treatment: _____

_____

_____

b. salon treatment: _____

_____

_____

_____

29. What causes the pigmentation pattern of poikiloderma of Cevattes? _____

_____

_____

_____

30. Neck skin is very _____ and susceptible to sun damage.

31. Skin that does not spring back immediately when you lift it and let go is suffering from

_____ .

32. Why would it be more accurate to call senile purpura "solar purpura"? _____

_____

33. What is Favre-Racouchot, and how is it treated? _____

_____

_____

_____

34. Define the term *keratosis*. _____

35. How would you recognize seborrheic keratoses on a client's skin? _____

_____

_____

_____

_____

_____

36. If actinic keratoses are not treated, they may become _____ .

    a. Describe actinic keratoses. _____

_____

_____

_____

    b. How are actinic keratoses treated? _____

_____

_____

_____

37. The primary cause of skin cancer is _____ .

38. How does smoking damage the skin?

   a. _____

   b. _____

   c. _____

   _____

   d. _____

39. How does excessive alcohol consumption affect the skin? _____

_____

_____

40. What is the single most important thing a client can do to protect the skin against premature

   aging? _____

TOPIC 3: Sunscreens

1. Sunscreens _____ or _____ ultraviolet rays.

2. Zinc oxide and titanium dioxide are known as _____ .

3. The main goal of early sunscreens was to prevent _____ .

4. SPF, or _____ , indicates _____

   _____ . It does *not* indicate how much _____ .

5. Everyone should wear sunscreen with an SPF of at least _____ and avoid _____

   _____ . For clients who spend a great deal of time in the sun or have histo-

   ries of skin cancer or sun-related problems, an SPF of _____ is recommended.

6. _____ sunscreens protect against both UVA and UVB rays.

7. Although zinc oxide and titanium dioxide are probably the most effective and least reactive

   sunscreen ingredients, they have one drawback for most consumers, which is _____

   _____ .

8. Sunscreens should be chosen according to a client's skin type; for oily and acne-prone skin, a

   _____ product should be chosen.

9. Water-resistant sunscreens have been tested to make sure they stay on the skin for up to

   _____ hours in the water, in rain, or in the presence of sweat.

10. It is important to educate your clients about the sun.

    a. A tan indicates _____ .

    b. Self-tanning products provide _____ protection against sun exposure.

    c. Sun exposure may occur at any time during _____ hours, even in the rain or on cloudy days.

    d. The sun is more damaging to the skin between the hours of _____ .

    e. Ultraviolet damage to the eyes, which can lead to _____ , can be prevented by _____ .

    f. Apply sunscreen at least _____ minutes before going outside and reapply every _____ minutes or so while you are in direct sunlight. Do *not* apply sunscreen after _____ .

    g. Sun damage cannot be fixed by _____ in any amount.

    h. Tanning beds use _____ to tan the skin and are not safe alternatives to the sun.

TOPIC 4: Analysis of Sun-Damaged Skin

1. Part of a skin analysis is lifting the skin with the thumb and forefinger and then letting go, to determine _____ .

2. As you work on a client's skin, look for any new, _____ -looking growths, an area that repeatedly _____ with no explanation, or lesions that do not _____ well. If you notice any of these, you should _____ .

3. Match the following terms with their definitions:

    _____ ulcerative carcinomas   a. most serious and deadly form of skin cancer

    _____ melanoma   b. common form of skin cancer that originates in the basal layer

    _____ sclerosing basal cell carcinoma   c. carcinoma that is dark and has melanocytes in the lesions

    _____ squamous cell carcinoma   d. carcinomas that are ulcerated and have an indented center

    _____ basal cell carcinoma   e. raised, crusty, or warty-looking carcinoma

_____ superficial basal cell carcinoma   f. carcinoma that looks like a scar and often occurs in the forehead

_____ pigmented basal cell carcinoma   g. carcinoma that looks like eczema

4. Basal cell carcinoma is most common in Fitzpatrick skin types _____ and in patients _____ years of age. It rarely _____ , or spreads to other organs.

5. Identify the different types of basal cell carcinoma described.

_____ pearl-like bump, flesh-colored or slightly pink, often with small capillaries running through it, generally painless

_____ looks like eczema; red, flat, scaly, frequently misdiagnosed

_____ looks like scar, often occurs in forehead, may linger over time

_____ has melanocytes involved in the lesions and is dark in color

_____ ulcerated, with indented center

6. Tissue samples are analyzed in a lab in a procedure called a _____ .

7. Name the treatments for basal cell carcinomas.

simple lesions: _____

recurrent/larger lesions: _____

more advanced cases: _____

8. The second most frequently diagnosed skin cancer is _____ .

   a. The appearance of this carcinoma is usually _____

   _____ .

   b. This cancer is caused by cumulative _____ and, to a lesser extent, by long-term exposure to _____ .

   c. People with _____ are more likely to develop this skin cancer.

   d. Squamous cell carcinoma can _____ and spread to other organs.

9. _____ is the number-one cancer among women aged 25 to 29.

   a. This cancer is also the _____ most common cancer in the United States.

   b. The cells responsible for this cancer are _____ .

   c. About _____ percent of people with melanoma die from it.

   d. One of the factors that may indicate a susceptibility to melanoma is the presence of many _____ , more than 50.

   e. People with certain types of nevi, called _____ nevi, are also more likely to get melanoma.

f. What are the ABCDs of melanoma? Briefly explain what each letter stands for.

A: _____

B: _____

C: _____

D: _____

g. Do all four of the preceding characteristics need to be present for a lesion to be a melanoma? _____

_____

h. How are melanomas treated? _____

_____

_____

TOPIC 5: Treatment Concepts for Sun-Damaged Skin

1. List six antiaging tips that should be included in salon treatments and shared with clients.

a. _____

b. _____

c. _____

d. _____

e. _____

f. _____

2. How do antioxidants help protect the skin? _____

_____

3. List some of the antioxidants commonly used in skin-care products.

a. _____

b. _____

c. _____

d. _____

e. _____

4. The use of _____ antioxidants may prevent different stages of the free radical reactions that lead to cell damage.

5. To protect the lipid barrier of the skin, clients should avoid exposure to:

    a. _____

    b. _____

    c. _____

    d. _____

    e. _____

    f. _____

6. A sign of alipidic skin is _____ pores.

7. To help reverse the surface signs of sun damage, regular use of _____ percent alphahy-droxy acid leave-on products is recommended.

8. How do alphahydroxy acids help the skin? _____

_____

_____

_____

9. Alphahydroxy acid products thin the epidermis and must be worn under _____

_____ .

10. Why are cleansers containing AHAs less effective than leave-on products? _____

_____

11. What is the minimum recommended pH of daily-use AHA products? _____

12. Without _____ , all the other ingredients in a skin-care regimen would be useless.

13. Identify each of the following ingredients as H=hydrating agent, A=antioxidant, S=soothing agent, E=emollient, or L=lipid.

    _____ borage oil

    _____ maritime pine bark extract

    _____ stearyl glycyrrhetinate

    _____ sodium hyaluronate

    _____ ceramides

    _____ proanthocyanidins

    _____ dimethicone

    _____ glycerin

_____ green tea extract

_____ cholesterol

_____ azulene extract

_____ sodium PCA

_____ petrolatum

_____ hyaluronic acid

TOPIC 6: Advanced Mature Skin Treatments

1. What is the purpose of a paraffin mask in a facial for mature skin? _____
_____

    a. How does an occlusive paraffin mask work? _____
_____
_____
_____

    b. Which types of clients should not receive this treatment? _____
_____

    c. What steps would be included in exfoliation and extraction? _____
_____
_____

    d. The treat-and-correct step consists of a _____ using a _____
or _____ current if applicable.

    e. Massage should be deeply _____ .

    f. An efficient way to apply the paraffin mask is to _____ .
_____
_____ .

    g. The mask step is complete when the mask has _____ .

2. Explain the action of a thermal mask. _____
_____
_____
_____

a. What is the purpose of a thermal mask? _____

_____

_____

b. Which types of clients should *not* receive this treatment? _____

_____

c. Why is it important to use all the mask powder specified by the manufacturer? _____

_____

d. A thermal mask is left on the skin for _____ minutes, or until the mask has

_____ .

3. What are the purposes of an antiaging firming treatment?

a. _____

b. _____

c. _____

4. Which product is used for exfoliation in an antiaging firming treatment? _____

a. Which products are massaged into the skin? _____

b. Which type of mask is applied? _____

_____

Discussion Questions

1. For your clients who love year-round outdoor activities, what advice can you give them about sun exposure?

2. If a client points out to you that aging is a natural process that cannot be stopped, what would your response be?

Word Review

actinic damage	cryosurgery	extrinsic aging factors	metastasize
basal cell carcinoma	curettage	Favre-Racouchot	Moh's surgery
biopsy	dermatoheliosis	genes	morphological
browtosis	elastosis	graft	mottling
crisscross wrinkling	electrodessication	hydroxy radicals	nasolabial folds
crosslinking	expression lines	lipid peroxides	nodulocystic

solar elastosis

solar urticaria

squamous cell
   carcinoma

subclinical
   inflammation

sun protection factor
   (SPF)

superficial basal cell
   carcinoma

superoxide

tactile roughness

ulcerative

ultra high frequency

UVA

UVB

water-resistant
   sunscreen

CHAPTER 22
Sensitive Skin: Morphology and Treatment

Date _____

Rating _____

Text pages: 340–355

TOPIC 1: Barrier Function and Sensitivity

1. Sensitive skin frequently suffers from an impaired _____ caused by a

   lack of _____ .

2. Gaps between the keratinocytes in the epidermis allow two adverse actions:

   a. _____

   b. _____

3. Sensitive skin becomes red, swollen, or inflamed when the _____ is activated.

TOPIC 2: Analysis of Sensitive Skin

1. Sensitive skin is more reactive to:

   a. _____

   b. _____

   c. _____

   d. _____

   e. _____

2. Under a magnifying lamp, sensitive skin has a _____ tone and appears very _____ .

3. What is touch-blanching? _____

_____

_____

4. Hereditary sensitive skin is usually very _____ in pigmentation and reacts to sunlight by

_____ .

5. Reactions to sun in darker, sensitive skins may include _____ .

6. Hives form when _____ is released by mast cells when the skin is irritated.

7. Define the term *dermatographism*. _____

_____

  a. For clients with this condition, you should avoid _____

_____

_____ .

8. When treating clients with sensitive skin:

  a. Avoid products containing _____ .

  b. Avoid aggressive treatments, such as _____

_____ .

  c. The skin may turn red more easily during treatments with _____

_____ .

  d. Using too many products and techniques will make it harder to _____

_____ .

  e. Products should have as few ingredients as possible and be tested for _____ .

9. _____ sensitivity is not permanent and is generally caused by environmental factors.

TOPIC 3: Irritants and Allergens

1. What is the basic difference between an irritant reaction and an allergic reaction? _____

_____

2. Define the term *irritant*. _____

_____

3. Allergic reactions are activated by the _____ system.

4. What is a second difference between allergies and irritant reactions? _____

_____

5. The first step in treating an allergic or irritant reaction is to _____ .

6. If you cannot determine what is causing an allergic or irritant reaction by examining the products a client is using, what should you do? _____

_____

_____

_____

7. If the skin is red and flaking, treatments should be _____

_____ .

    a. Inflamed skin can be cooled with _____ .

    b. Allergic reactions may be treated with topical _____ .

8. Identify which of the following substances are frequent allergens or frequent irritants, or both:
A=allergen, I=irritant, AI=both.

    _____ fragrances

    _____ roll-off exfoliators

    _____ essential oils

    _____ lanolin

    _____ PABA sunscreen

    _____ AHAs

    _____ resorcinol

    _____ benzoyl peroxide

    _____ strong detergent cleansers

    _____ nail products

    _____ drying clay masks

TOPIC 4: Rosacea

1. Rosacea most often affects these general groups:

    a. those with _____ skin types

    b. those of _____ descent

    c. _____ age groups

2. Although rosacea was once considered a form of acne, now it is thought to be a _____ disorder.

3. What are often the first signs of rosacea? _____

4. Aggravating factors for rosacea are such vasodilators as:

   a. _____

   b. _____

   c. _____

   d. _____

   e. _____

5. Rosacea should be treated in the same way as _____ skin.

TOPIC 5: Aging and the Sensitive Skin

1. In sensitive skin, _____ and _____ are closer to the surface.

2. List five tips for clients with sensitive skin.

   a. _____

   b. _____

   c. _____

   d. _____

   e. _____

3. Traditional soaps cause _____ loss.

4. An ultrasonic steamer produces a _____ rather than steam and is recommended for sensitive skin.

5. Sensitive skin is more likely to be irritated by _____ sunscreens and more tolerant of _____ sunscreens such as zinc oxide and titanium dioxide.

6. AHAs and other exfoliants should never be used on skin that is _____

   _____ .

7. Can essential oils play a role in sensitive skin treatments? _____

8. What is the purpose of a salon treatment for sensitive skin? _____

   a. Cleanser should be _____ and _____ and should be applied with _____ .

b. If steam must be used, the steamer should be at least _____ inches away from the face and its use limited to _____ minutes.

c. After performing gentle extraction, apply _____ for several minutes.

d. Before massage, apply a hydrating fluid or light cream containing _____ ingredients.

e. Before applying a mask, you may cover the face with gauze and glide _____ over the skin.

f. For sensitive skin, a _____ mask will hydrate and cool the skin.

9. You should keep a home-maintenance program for a client with sensitive skin as _____ as possible.

10. The morning routine should include:

a. _____

_____

b. _____

c. _____

d. _____

e. _____

11. The nighttime routine should include:

a. _____

b. _____

c. _____

d. _____

e. _____

f. _____

Word Review

dermatographism

touch-blanching

CHAPTER 23
Hyperpigmentation: Morphology and Treatment

Date _____

Rating _____

Text pages: 356–363

TOPIC 1: Analysis

1. List the six signs of hyperpigmentation you should look for during a skin analysis.

    a. _____

    b. _____

    c. _____

    d. _____

    e. _____

    f. _____

2. What is mottling? _____

_____

3. Mottling is the very first sign of _____ .

    a. Home treatment for mottling consists of applying _____

    _____ along with sunscreen.

4. Liver spots, or _____ , are actually spots of _____

    _____ .

5. _____ is any form of splotchy hyperpigmentation but is most often seen in women in

    the form of a pregnancy mask. It is related to _____ fluctuation and therapies.

6. The esthetician can treat a client with melasma but should also _____ _____ .

7. Even if hyperpigmentation is corrected, the melanocytes that overproduced the melanin will always have that tendency and are easily _____ .

8. Clients with hyperpigmentation must make a strong commitment to avoid _____ , even when they are wearing sunscreen.

9. People with _____ skin are more likely to have hyperpigmentation. Why? _____

_____

_____

10. Hyperpigmentation may be caused by _____ lesions.

11. Overly aggressive exfoliation and other treatments stimulate the _____ and worsen a case of hyperpigmentation.

TOPIC 2: Treatment for Hyperpigmentation

1. How are AHAs used in the treatment of hyperpigmentation? _____

_____

_____

2. What are melanin suppressive agents? _____

_____

3. The FDA has approved only one ingredient as a melanin suppressant, _____ . It is available in these concentrations:

   _____ percent   standard prescription

   _____ percent   physician-dispensed formulas

   _____ percent   OTC

4. Nonprescription ingredients called _____ by their manufacturers include kojic acid, ascorbyl glucosamine, asafetida extract, and others.

5. Many practitioners feel the most effective form of lightening agents is _____ .

6. Lightening and brightening agents are best used in conjunction with _____

_____ . The ingredient usually used for this purpose is _____ .

7. List the steps of a morning home-care routine for hyperpigmented skin.

   a. _____

   b. _____

   c. _____

      _____

   d. _____

      _____

8. How does the nighttime routine differ from the morning routine? _____

   _____

9. What is the key treatment in salon procedures for hyperpigmentation? Why? _____

   _____

   _____

   _____

10. AHAs used in salon treatments should not exceed _____ percent concentration or have
    a pH lower than _____ .

11. An alternative to AHAs is _____ . For more stubborn cases, exfoliation with
    _____ or _____ may be used.

CHAPTER 24
Acne: Morphology and Treatment

Date _____

Rating _____

Text pages: 364–389

TOPIC 1: What Causes Acne?

1. The main causes of acne are:

    a. _____

    b. _____

2. The hereditary factor in acne is known as _____ , which means that _____
_____
_____ .

3. Corneum cells are on the surface of the skin and also form the lining of the _____ .

4. Clients with very _____ skin have a stronger tendency toward severe acne.

5. Enlarged pores in oily areas are caused by _____
_____ .

6. Match the following terms with their definitions or descriptions:

    _____ blackheads   a. follicular canal

    _____ infundibulum   b. lesion that becomes red; acne papule

    _____ oxidation   c. term used for closed comedones

    _____ whiteheads   d. term used to describe deeper acne lesion

    _____ microcomedo   e. process in which sebum darkens when
                                                  exposed to oxygen

_____ inflammatory acne lesion   f. very deep pocket of infection, with pus

_____ P. acnes   g. open comedones

_____ cyst   h. plug of oil and sebum in the follicle

_____ nodule   i. swelling inside a follicle

_____ comedo   j. beginning of plug formation that is too
                                  small and too deep in follicle to be seen

_____ perifollicular inflammation   k. bacteria that cause acne vulgaris

7. A comedo begins when cells build up on the walls and bottom of the follicle and mix with

_____ .

8. Name and describe the two types of comedones.

a. _____

_____

_____

b. _____

_____

_____

9. *Propionibacterium acnes* are _____ bacteria, which cannot survive in the presence of
oxygen.

10. Why do *P. acnes* bacteria thrive in acne-prone skin? _____

_____

11. Describe the formation of an inflammatory acne lesion. _____

_____

_____

_____

_____

_____

12. What is pus? _____

_____

13. What is the main difference between papules and pustules? _____
_____

14. Which type of comedo is more likely to lead to papule or pustule formation? Why? _____
_____
_____

15. Deeper acne lesions, sometimes called _____ , can be felt easily under the skin.

16. What is cystic acne? Can it be treated in the salon? _____
_____
_____

17. One of the characteristics of severe acne is depressed scars or _____ .

18. How are sebaceous filaments different from open comedones? _____
_____
_____

19. Two home-care products useful for clients with sebaceous filaments are _____
and _____ .

TOPIC 2: Hormones and Acne

1. Male hormones, or androgens, play a role in acne in two ways:

    a. _____
    b. _____

2. Hormones are secreted in substantial amounts beginning at _____ , when _____
enlarge and pores appear.

3. Home-care programs for young clients with acne should be kept simple and specific because
_____ .

4. Home-care products for teenagers with problem skin should include:

    a. _____
    b. _____
    c. _____
    d. _____

5. Females are more likely to suffer from adult acne than males largely because of _____

_____ .

6. Define the following types of acne:

premenstrual acne   _____

_____

comedonal acne   _____

inflammatory acne   _____

_____

7. Products that cause follicle inflammation and papule formation in some individuals are called

_____ . _____ products cause or contribute to cell buildup and the formation of

comedones.

8. Salon treatment for premenstrual acne should include:

a. _____

b. _____

TOPIC 3: Stress Factors

1. How does stress lead to acne breakouts? _____

_____

_____

TOPIC 4: Foods and Acne

1. What is the relationship between food and acne? _____

_____

_____

TOPIC 5: Cosmetics, Skin-Care Products, and Acne

1. Comedogenic emollients aggravate acne or the formation of comedones by:

a. _____

_____

b. _____

2. Why are powders and blushes considered very comedogenic? _____

_____

_____

TOPIC 6: Grades of Acne

1. Describe the four grades of acne.

      Grade 1: _____

      Grade 2: _____

      Grade 3: _____

                   _____

      Grade 4: _____

                   _____

                   _____

2. Dermatological treatment is necessary for clients with grades _____ . An esthetician can support medical treatment with _____ .

3. What is a lesion count? _____

_____

TOPIC 7: Concepts of Acne Management

1. List six tips for the effective salon and home treatment of acne.

      a. _____

      b. _____

      c. _____

      d. _____

      e. _____

      f. _____

2. Acne _____ is caused by skin-care and cosmetic products.

3. Products that may cause or aggravate acne cosmetica include:

      a. _____

      b. _____

      c. _____

4. Clients who are both acne prone and concerned about sun damage and aging should use products that:

    a. _____

    b. _____

5. The term *oil free* is misleading because many oil-free products _____

_____ .

6. Foaming cleansers for very oily skin may contain such medication as _____ or

    _____ .

7. Toners for oily and acne-prone skin may contain _____ as an antibacterial, and toners may contain chamomile extract or aloe as _____ agents.

8. Keratolytics dissolve _____ .

9. Antibacterial agents that are used to kill *P. acnes* bacteria include:

    a. _____

    b. _____

    c. _____

10. How do AHAs help control *P. acnes* bacteria? _____

_____

11. AHA use can be reserved for papules and pustules, a type of treatment called _____ .

12. Clients and estheticians must make a point of treating not only visible inflammatory lesions but also _____ . The solution is to use an _____ on all areas of the face to prevent comedone formation as well as a stronger keratolytic on individual lesions.

13. Overcleansing the face can lead to _____ .

14. The skin should never be washed more than _____ times a day.

15. Environmental aggravators of acne include:

    a. _____

    b. _____

    c. _____

16. Is sun exposure helpful for acne? _____

_____

_____

17. Stress contributes to acne largely because of the _____ it causes.

TOPIC 8: Analysis and Treatment of Problem Skin

1. What are signs of acne excoriée? _____

_____

2. Before examining the client's skin, cleanse it with _____ .

3. Describe the morning home-care routine and products for a client with acne-prone skin.

cleansing _____

_____

_____

toner/freshener _____

_____

_____

AHA _____

_____

_____

_____

sunscreen/day cream _____

_____

_____

eye cream _____

makeup _____

_____

_____

_____

4. Describe the evening home-care routine and products for this client.

makeup removal _____

_____

second cleansing _____

_____

toner _____

AHA _____

medication/drying agent _____

_____

hydration fluid _____

_____

eye cream _____

5. When applying most home-care products, it is important to avoid the _____ area.

6. Which type of masks are recommended for acne skins? _____

_____

_____

_____

7. When clients pick at their skin while asleep, suggest that they _____ .

8. Match the following terms with their definitions or brand names:

_____ Retin-A   a. adapalene

_____ Differin   b. combination of erythromycin and benzoyl peroxide

_____ doxycycline   c. only drug routinely effective against cystic acne

_____ Accutane   d. topical antibiotic

_____ erythromycin   e. prescription keratolytic drug

_____ Benzamycin   f. oral antibiotic often prescribed for grade 3 acne

9. Tretinoin is a _____ and works by normalizing the exfoliation of the follicular lining.

10. The side effects of tretinoin include:

a. _____

b. _____

c. _____

d. _____

e. _____

11. Clients using tretinoin should avoid irritants and other exfoliating and stimulating products, and skin treated with tretinoin should never be _____ .

12. Name three other keratolytics similar to tretinoin.

a. _____

b. _____

c. _____

13. What is the role of topical antibiotics in acne treatments? _____
_____

14. What is the role of oral antibiotics in acne treatments? _____
_____

15. How is Accutane used in acne treatment? _____
_____

16. Which precautions must be taken with clients using Accutane? _____
_____
_____
_____

17. Ideally, clients with problem skin should use their home-care products for _____ before their first salon treatments.

18. In salon procedures, comedones are loosened through _____ , _____ , or a combination of both.

19. How do disincrustation products work? _____
_____
_____

20. When treating acne skin, _____ should not be applied, because it can construct the follicle openings.

21. Disincrustation with steam generally lasts about _____ minutes. For skin that is thicker, oilier, or more impacted, _____ current may also be used unless contraindicated.

22. Briefly describe the three methods of extracting comedones.

a. _____

b. _____

c. _____

_____

23. What is the purpose of a lancet? _____

_____

_____

24. How should a lancet be held during use? _____

_____

25. The extraction part of a procedure should not last longer than _____ minutes.

26. What should follow extraction?

a. _____

_____

b. _____

_____

c. _____

27. How is high-frequency current useful in acne treatment?

a. _____

b. _____

c. _____

28. What is fulguration? _____

_____

_____

29. Masks for acne skin are generally _____ -based and contain exfoliants and

_____ agents.

30. Why should massage be avoided on acne-prone skin? _____

_____

TOPIC 9: Step-by-Step Treatment for Problem Skin

1. What are the purposes of a problem skin treatment?

   a. _____

   b. _____

   c. _____

   d. _____

2. Describe what is done during the second cleansing. _____

   _____

   _____

   _____

   _____

3. The skin should be damp for extraction, which should begin in the _____ .

4. Define the term *saponifiers*. _____

   _____

5. Before high frequency is applied, the face should be covered with a(n) _____ .

6. Although clay masks are generally used on acne skins, for sensitive oily skins you may use a(n) _____ mask.

7. Clients with problem skin should have salon treatments about every _____ until the skin has cleared.

Discussion Questions

1. Clients with acne, especially those who have suffered with the problem for many years, are sometimes very sensitive about their skin. Describe the best way to approach such clients.

2. How do acnegenic and comedogenic products differ? Can you name examples of each?

3. If a client asks you if there is a cure for acne, what would your answer be?

Word Review

acne cosmetica

acne detergicans

acnegenic

blackheads

comedo

comedonal acne

inflammatory acne

inflammatory acne

lesion

infundibulum

microcomedo

noninflammatory

perifollicular

inflammation

pocks

premenstrual acne

retention
hyperkeratosis

sebaceous filaments

spot treatment

CHAPTER 25
Ethnic Skin: Morphology and Treatment

Date _____

Rating _____

Text pages: 390–395

Introduction

1. List the ethnic skin types.

    a. _____

    b. _____

    c. _____

    d. _____

2. The chief distinction between ethnic and Caucasian skin is the _____ in the skin.

3. Ethnic skin is generally more protected against, but not invulnerable to, _____ .

TOPIC 1: Black Skin

1. A common misperception about black skin is that it is always _____ .

2. Black skin differs from Caucasian skin in two respects:

    a. _____

    b. _____

3. Match the following terms with their definitions or descriptions.

_____ leukoderma   a. thickening of the horny layer of the epidermis

_____ hyperkeratosis   b. scarring reaction more commonly seen in black
                                     skin

_____ vitiligo   c. partial or total absence of pigment in the skin

_____ keloids   d. hyperpigmentation due to hormones

_____ melasma   e. a form of hypopigmentation

4. Hyperkeratosis leads to a higher rate of cell turnover, so black skin _____
dead skin cells more readily, giving the skin surface an _____ appearance.

5. Skin cancer is less prevalent in black skin, which is _____ and produces more

_____ .

6. Black skin is often prone to hypopigmentation disorders such as _____ and
_____ , which are characterized by partial or total absence of pigment.

7. Hyperpigmentation in black skin may occur as a response to:

    a. _____

    b. _____

    c. _____

    d. _____

8. Why should the esthetician be particularly careful when performing extractions on black skin?

_____

9. Melasma and chloasma are often induced by:

    a. _____

    b. _____

    c. _____

10. How does erythema appear in black skin, and how should it be treated in the salon? _____

_____

11. Explain how keloids are formed. _____

_____

_____

12. Because black skin has a greater tendency to form keloids, it could be risky to perform _____ on postacne scars or to use a _____ or _____ .

13. Why does black skin not age as quickly as Caucasian skin? _____

_____

_____

14. If pigment lighteners are used carelessly, _____ may result. When using these products at home, clients should be cautioned to:

a. _____

b. _____

c. _____

TOPIC 2: Asian Skin

1. Asian skin is the most _____ .

2. Instead of exfoliating Asian skin with higher-level AHAs and BHAs, Retin-A, and other aggressive substances, better choices would be:

a. _____

b. _____

c. _____

3. For Asian clients, _____ and _____ are considered the worst facial trauma.

4. The most important product an Asian client can use is _____

_____ .

5. Titanium dioxide has _____ as well as sunscreen properties and is appealing to Asian clients for that reason.

6. Because Asian skin is sometimes prone to develop _____ after injury, any aggressive treatments should be performed with caution.

TOPIC 3: Hispanic and Native American Skin

1. Hispanic and Native American skin is predisposed to many of the same problems as _____ _____ skin.

2. One difference between Hispanic/Native American skin and black/Asian skin is that if AHA or BHA treatment causes hyperpigmentation, it _____

   _____ .

3. _____ skin probably has the strongest hair growth and root system, which may make _____ more difficult than on Caucasian skin.

4. Hispanic and Native American skin is often _____ and has more _____ .

5. Care must be taken during extractions because _____ may form around the extracted lesions.

6. The common characteristic of all ethnic skin is its tendency to _____ .

Discussion Questions

1. If you have worked with different ethnic skins, is it your impression that some present more challenges than others?

2. Why do black and Asian skins age more slowly than Caucasian skin?

Word Review

leukoderma

CHAPTER 26
Exfoliation

Date _____

Rating _____

Text pages: 396–417

Introduction

1. Define exfoliation in terms of skin care. _____
   _____
   _____

2. Name two factors that slow or inhibit the natural sloughing-off of skin cells.

   a. _____
      _____

   b. _____

3. Exfoliation increases the rate of natural _____ . As we age, this cycle changes from
   _____ days to _____ days or more.

4. Overly aggressive exfoliation may destroy the skin's _____ .

TOPIC 1: Mechanical versus Chemical Exfoliation

1. Name the two types of exfoliation, define them, and list some examples.

Type of Exfoliation	Definition	Examples

2. How do chemical exfoliants work? _____

_____ .

TOPIC 2: Mechanical Exfoliation

1. Granular scrubs made with _____ provide a gentler, more enhanced exfoliation than scrubs made with grains.

2. Scrub movements can be made smoother and easier by simultaneously using _____ .
   On skin that is thick or leathery, you may use a _____ .

3. List three precautions to follow with scrubs.

   a. _____

   b. _____

   c. _____

   _____

4. Explain how gommage is used to exfoliate the skin. _____

_____

_____

5. Some gommages use _____ as the rolling agent; some include a cellular dissolving agent, such as a(n) _____ .

6. Rub-off gommages are contraindicated for clients with:

    a. _____

    b. _____

    c. _____

7. List four precautions to follow with gommages.

    a. _____

    _____

    b. _____

    c. _____

    _____

    d. _____

    _____

8. Gommage should not be used with _____ , which makes the gommage gummy and almost impossible to rub off.

9. How should gommage be rubbed off? _____

_____

_____

10. Gommage residue should be wiped off with _____ .

11. Explain the process of microdermabrasion. _____

_____

_____

12. When a microdermabrasion wand is passed over the skin, it does two things:

    a. _____

    b. _____

13. The single most important part of performing microdermabrasion safely and effectively is

    _____ .

14. List six precautions that must be followed with microdermabrasion.

a. _____

b. _____

c. _____

_____

d. _____

e. _____

f. _____

TOPIC 3: Chemical Exfoliation

1. In general terms, estheticians perform exfoliations and physicians perform _____ .

2. Esthetic procedures affect the _____ layer of the skin. Any procedure that removes cells below this layer is considered _____ .

3. Match the following terms with their definitions or descriptions.

_____ deep peels

_____ dermabrasion

_____ superficial peels

_____ medium-depth peels

_____ phenol

_____ microdermabrasion

_____ ablate

_____ trichloroacetic acid

a. highly acidic chemical generally reserved for deeply wrinkled skin and severe sun damage

b. mechanical form of superficial peeling

c. peels in which the entire epidermis is removed

d. to remove

e. peels in which only dead cells are removed from the epidermis

f. surgical technique using a rotating wire brush to physically remove skin tissue

g. chemical used in medium-depth peels

h. surgical peels that remove tissue well into the papillary dermis

4. AHAs, BHAs, sulfur, and resorcinol are used to perform _____ peels.

5. Laser resurfacing removes _____ tissue.

6. What is dermabrasion most often used for? _____

_____

7. Explain how alphahydroxy acids work on the skin. _____

_____

_____

8. Most salon exfoliations use AHAs in _____ percent concentration, and _____ is the most commonly used AHA.

9. How do AHA treatments help the following conditions?

acne/clogged pores   _____

_____

_____

_____

_____

hyperpigmentation   _____

_____

aging/sun damage   _____

_____

dehydration   _____

_____

_____

rough-textured skin   _____

_____

_____

10. Clients who take the following drugs should avoid AHA treatments:

a. _____

_____

b. _____

11. Clients with the following conditions should *not* receive AHA treatments:

a. _____

b. _____

_____

c. _____

d. _____

e. _____

f. _____

g. _____

h. _____

i. _____

12. Clients receiving AHA treatments must agree to _____ during the treatment and for several weeks afterward.

13. Before receiving salon AHA treatments, clients should use _____ percent AHA at home for at least 2 weeks.

14. A home-care AHA program should be tailored to the client's skin type and condition. Fill in the blanks with terms from the following list. (Please note that not all terms are used.)

3.0	at least 30	hydrator
3.5	antioxidants	lower eyelid
7	drying alcohol	lower pH
10	emollients	salicylic acid
15	fragrance	soaps
15 or higher	green tea extract	upper eyelid
30	higher pH	

a. The client should *not* use _____ or other alkaline products.

b. Except for very oily skin, toner should be free of _____ and _____ and should not be stimulating.

c. AHA products for dry skin often contain more _____ ; for oily and acne-prone skins _____ ; for sensitive skin slightly _____ or soothing agents such as _____ .

d. According to the Cosmetic Ingredient Review Board (CIR), AHA home-care products should not exceed _____ percent concentration or have a pH lower than _____ . Salon products should not exceed _____ percent concentration or have a pH lower than _____ .

e. AHA products should *never* be applied on the _____ ; around the eye area, only products designed for the eye area, with a _____ , should be used.

f. The CIR stipulates that a sunscreen with SPF _____ be used daily.

g. A _____ worn over the AHA product at night helps replenish moisture lost from the exfoliation process.

15. An AHA exfoliation should never be performed at _____ of a facial treatment.

16. Clients receiving AHA treatments should be urged to commit to a series of _____
_____ .

17. After the initial series of AHA treatments, maintenance treatments may be scheduled how often? _____

18. The skin may return to its former condition if the client _____
_____

19. How should salon AHA treatments be coordinated with facial procedures for clients:

with sensitive skin?   _____

whose skin is not sensitive? _____
                              _____

20. Exfoliation with Jessner's solution, resorcinol paste, TCA, and other similar products is appropriate for clients with _____
_____

21. Match the following terms with their definitions or descriptions.

_____ BHAs   a. strong acid with many serious side effects

_____ resorcinol paste   b. solution of lactic acid, salicylic acid, and resorcinol in ethanol solvent

_____ frosting   c. removal of dead skin cells at the smallest level

_____ salicylic acid   d. skin that turns white in patches after intense chemical exfoliation

_____ Jessner's solution e. cream exfoliant used to treat hyperpigmentation

_____ TCA   f. most commonly used BHA

_____ microdesquamation   g. lipophilic exfoliant used alone or alternated with AHAs

22. A Jessner's exfoliation is considered superficial because _____
_____ , but it should not be performed unless the esthetician _____
_____ .

23. Jessner's is appropriate for which skin conditions?

    a. _____

    b. _____

    c. _____

    d. _____

24. Which effects can the client expect during and after treatment with Jessner's solution?

    during: _____

    after: _____

    _____

25. What is the purpose of prepping solution in a Jessner's exfoliation? _____

_____

26. Resorcinol paste is similar to Jessner's in application, but it is more _____ and is used to

treat _____ .

27. A controversial exfoliant whose use is limited in some states to physicians is _____

_____ .

28. BHAs are _____ , which means they have the ability to dissolve oil-based accumulated

dead cells.

29. Salicylic acids are effective skin-care agents in many ways.

    a. Salicylic acids have _____ , _____ , and _____ properties.

    b. They also reduce _____ that contribute to thick, clogged skin.

    c. They may suppress the bacteria _____ , which contribute to pustule formation.

    d. They are _____ , which means they can dissolve comedones.

30. Salicylic is considered a particularly safe exfoliant, because there is no evidence of _____

_____ .

31. Salicylic acid should be applied at intervals of _____ , and use of other _____

agents should be terminated a few days before a professional salicylic acid treatment. Accutane

should be discontinued _____ before treatment.

32. List the precautions that must be followed with BHA treatments.

    a. _____

    _____

    b. _____

c. _____

d. _____

e. _____

f. _____

g. _____

h. _____

_____

TOPIC 4: Enzymes

1. Define the term *enzyme.* _____

_____

2. The enzymes most commonly used in cosmetics are derived from _____ .

3. How are enzymes applied? _____

_____

4. Super oxide dismutase, or SOD, is an enzyme that _____

_____ .

5. Enzymes are also used in cosmetics to reduce the _____ .

6. From what are these enzymes derived?

papain   _____

bromelain   _____

pancreatin   _____

7. Enzymes come in the form of a _____ and are mixed with water to produce the mask paste.

8. List the precautions that must be followed when using enzymes.

a. _____

b. _____

c. _____

d. _____

_____

1. What is the purpose of an AHA treatment? _____

_____

    a. Toner may be applied after cleansing if the skin is *not* _____ , but it is best not to use it on the client's _____ visit.

    b. The next step after toner is to _____ and _____ the head slightly so that gel will not roll into the eyes.

    c. AHA gel is applied with _____ to the center panel of the face, then in a very thin coat under the eyes, no closer than _____ to the lashes.

    d. The client should expect to feel a _____ sensation after AHA gel is applied. If the client asks you to remove the gel, you should _____ .

    e. Typical 30 percent salon-use AHA gels are left on the face for _____ minutes.

    f. AHA gel should be removed first with _____ , then with _____ _____ .

    g. After the gel is removed, spray the face with _____ , not _____ .

    h. As the last step, apply _____ and _____ .

2. What is the purpose of a BHA treatment? _____

_____

    a. As part of client preparation, be sure to obtain the client's signature on a _____ _____ .

    b. When performing a BHA treatment, you should not perform any other treatments, including _____ and _____ .

    c. After cleansing the face and applying freshener, the next step is to _____ _____ . What kind of product might be used for this step? _____

    d. A degreaser is necessary because BHAs are _____ , or oil loving.

    e. The BHA solution may be applied in the crow's feet area, but no closer to the eye than _____ .

    f. What should the client expect to feel when BHA is applied? _____ _____

    g. The BHA is _____ , meaning that it discontinues its action within a given time.

h. What is the next step following removal of the BHA? _____
_____

3. What is the purpose of an enzyme treatment? _____
_____

    a. As in the BHA treatment, the client should be asked to sign a _____ .

    b. Enzyme paste is applied to the face, neck, and décolleté with a _____ .

    c. An enzyme mask must be kept _____ for the time it is on the client's face, up to
_____ minutes. You may direct light _____ toward the face from a distance
to keep the enzyme activated.

    d. Remove the mask immediately with cool water if you notice _____ .

Word Review

bromelain	epidermolysis	mechanical	resorcinol paste
chemical exfoliation	frosting	exfoliation	superficial peeling
comedolidic	gommage	medium-depth peels	trichloroacetic acid
deep peels	Jessner's solution	papain	(TCA)
dermabrasion	lipophilic	phenol	

CHAPTER 27
Holistic/Alternative Skin Care

Date_____

Rating_____

Text pages: 418–425

Introduction

1. _____ medicine focuses more on the symptoms than the causes of disease.

2. A _____ approach to health encompasses all modalities of complementary wellness practices.

TOPIC 1: Psychological Benefits of Holistic Practices

1. A holistic esthetic treatment includes both proper technique and a less tangible but equally important factor, _____ .

TOPIC 2: Mind-Body Connection

1. Milk is beneficial when applied to the skin, as in a bath, because it contains _____ _____ .

2. The most healing part of a treatment lies in the power of the practitioner's _____ .

3. The common feature of the various holistic therapies is _____ , which is transmitted by the esthetician toward the client.

TOPIC 3: Methods of Holistic Therapy

1. Acupressure and acupuncture are based on the _____ .

    a. Explain the energy pathways on which acupressure and acupuncture are based. _____

    _____

    _____

    _____

    _____

    b. How do acupressure and acupuncture differ? _____

    _____

    _____

    c. These therapies are considered _____ as well as healing.

2. In _____ , essential oils are used for their healing and rejuvenating effects.

    a. Essential oils may be added to _____ for massage.

    b. Essential oils are known to affect the _____ in the brain.

3. Match the following terms to their definitions or descriptions:

    _____ reflexology

                              a. massage therapist's hands rebalance overall energy in client's body

    _____ Trager method   b. dripping oil into the "third eye"

    _____ Lomi Lomi   c. gentle massage of the cranium

    _____ Ayurvedic   d. massage method practiced mostly in Hawaii

    _____ polarity therapy   e. finger pressure therapy

    _____ trigger point myotherapy   f. means "the science of life"

    _____ shiodara   g. body is gently rocked to produce positive energy stimulation

    _____ Reiki   h. pressure is applied to the feet or hands

    _____ craniosacral massage   i. concentrates on relieving myofacial pain

    _____ shiatsu   j. resembles laying-on of hands

4. Ayurvedic originated over 5,000 years ago in _____ .

5. What are doshas? _____

    _____

a. Define the following three doshas.

vata   _____

_____

pitta _____

_____

kapha _____

_____

_____

6. What treatment methods are employed in Ayurvedic?

a. _____

b. _____

c. _____

d. _____

e. _____

f. _____

g. _____

7. What is the goal of craniosacral massage? _____

_____

_____

8. Describe the goal and technique of Lomi Lomi. _____

_____

_____

9. What is polarity therapy, and who developed it?_____

_____

_____

10. _____ is a healing technique that feels like energy flowing through the practitioner's

hands. Its goal is to _____ .

11. What is the concept behind reflexology? _____

_____

_____

12. Who was Dr. William Fitzgerald? _____

_____

13. Shiatsu is similar to acupressure, with the added component of _____ .

    a. What are the origins of shiatsu? _____

    _____

    b. How is shiatsu performed? _____

    _____

14. The Trager method is a mobility treatment that results in _____

_____ , which leaves the client feeling _____ .

15. Trigger point therapy applies pressure to trigger points in the _____ , _____ , and

_____ .

16. _____ includes vegetarian and macrobiotic diets, tai chi, yoga, meditation, and other

practices.

17. It is important to remember that many alternative therapies require _____

_____ to practice.

Short Essay/Discussion Question

1. In your own words, define what *holistic* means to you.

2. Have you practiced or experienced any of the holistic therapies described in this chapter? If you
have, what were the effects? Which ones would you be interested in mastering?

Word Review

Ayurvedic	Lomi Lomi	Reiki	Trager method
craniosacral massage	polarity therapy	shiodara	

CHAPTER 28
Advanced Home Care

Date _____

Rating _____

Text pages: 426–437

TOPIC 1: Understanding Your Client

1. Part of the job of understanding your client is staying up to date on all popular _____
   _____ skin-care products.

2. One of the most important breakthroughs in skin care, and one that has attracted the interest
   of many consumers, is retinol delivered through _____ technology.

   a. Retinol is considered a highly effective _____ product.

TOPIC 2: Advanced Product Types and Features

1. List the general features of these advanced home-care products.

   deep pore cleanser

   a. _____

   b. _____

   c. _____

   home-care-strength exfoliation

   a. _____

   b. _____

   c. _____

specific-use serum

a. _____

b. _____

c. _____

eye cream/gel

a. _____

b. _____

c. _____

neck cream

a. _____

b. _____

c. _____

premakeup serum or ampoule

a. _____

b. _____

c. _____

TOPIC 3: Introducing Advanced Products to the Client

1. At which two points in a service does the majority of client education about product choices and uses take place?

a. _____

b. _____

2. Specific products should not be mentioned by name during the _____ , but rather

_____ .

TOPIC 4: The Home-Care Treatment Form

1. For a client who does not want a complicated routine, begin by recommending only the most important products that will produce _____ .

TOPIC 5: Advanced/Enhanced Selling

1. A successful, truly effective skin-care program for any client integrates both _____ and _____ treatments.

2. Selling should not be seen as just another way to make money; it is the esthetician's _____ .

3. What is the best way to handle the fact that many skin-care products and programs are expensive for your clients? _____

_____

4. You will make a more convincing and effective salesperson if you yourself _____ _____ .

5. Because you should never overstate the benefits of a product, it is better to use words such as _____ or _____ instead of *correct*.

TOPIC 6: Sample Advanced Product Plans

1. What is ingredient synergy? _____

_____ .

2. The rate at which the skin ages is determined by _____ aging and _____ .

3. What are the goals of a skin-care system for aging and environmentally damaged skin?

_____

_____

4. _____ ingredients help the skin regenerate fibroblastic activity.

5. _____ ingredients are beneficial to skin experiencing a decrease in hormone activity.

6. The skin-care system for sensitive skin is ideal for clients who have had _____ and _____ treatments.

7. What are the goals of a skin-care system for sensitive skin? _____

_____

_____

_____

8. What are the goals of a skin-care system for problem or acne skin? _____

_____

_____

9. The ingredients in a system for problem skin focus on _____ and _____ proper-

ties, with _____ and _____ to soften and moisturize.

10. List the benefits for aging skin of the following biologicals:

collagen _____

elastin _____

DNA _____

11. Match the following phyto extracts with their benefits for aging skin.

_____ pinecone

_____ turmeric

_____ calendula

_____ ginseng

_____ rosemary

_____ thyme

_____ geranium

a. stimulating, regenerative, antiseptic, antioxidant, anti-inflammatory

b. revitalizing, fortifying, toning

c. regenerative, astringent, calming

d. strengthening (capillaries), smoothing, decongesting

e. astringent (toning), stimulating, antiseptic

f. regenerative, soothing, antiseptic

g. activating, stimulating, regenerative, calming, antimicrobial

12. Match the following lipids with their benefits for aging skin.

_____ rice bran oil

_____ squalane (olives)

_____ soybean oil

_____ orange roughy oil

a. moisturizing, lubricating, soothing, regenerative

b. fatty acids omega-3 and -6 to soften and nourish

c. emollient, antioxidant, moisturizing, linoleic acid

d. soothing, estrogenic, fatty acids, vitamins A, E, K, nourishing

13. Match the following ingredients with the following list.

allantoin	honey	vitamin B6
beta-glucans	hyaluronic acid	vitamin C
glycerin	sodium PCA	vitamin E
glycoproteins	vitamin A	

_____ humectant (moisturizing), softening

_____ antioxidant, regenerative, stimulating, collagen synthesis

_____ humectant, desensitizing

_____ regenerative, softening, protective, moisturizing, restorative

_____ moisturizing, regenerative, conditioning, humectant, softening

_____ prevents tissue degeneration, antioxidant, normalizing, firming, regenerative, fortifying

_____ emollient, soothing, moisturizing

_____ emollient, regenerative, soothing, desensitizing

_____ antioxidant, nourishing, soothing, hydrating

_____ enhance cell metabolism, boosting cells' oxygen consumption

_____ moisture binding, softening

14. List the benefits for sensitive skin offered by the following biologicals:

collagen   _____

elastin   _____

DNA   _____

15. In the following chart, indicate which benefits each phyto extract provides for sensitive skin.

Phyto extract	anti-inflammatory	astringent	soothing	stimulating	healing
lavender					
arnica					
chamomile					
hyssop					
comfrey					
cucumber					
hypericum					
mallow					
grape					

16. List the lipids used in products for sensitive skin.

    a. _____

    b. _____

    c. _____

    d. _____

    e. _____

    f. _____

17. All the lipids you listed previously have emollient properties. Which one also has anti-inflammatory and decongesting properties? _____ Which one is desensitizing? _____

18. Vitamin _____ benefits sensitive skin by firming and supporting epidermal cell turnover.

19. Identify each of the following botanicals, then locate it in the following word search puzzle.

_____ analgesic, antiseptic, cooling, calming

_____ wound-healing, anti-inflammatory

_____ lymphatic stimulant, purifying, antiseptic

_____ anti-inflammatory, cooling, sedative, antiseptic, astringent

_____ purifying, regenerative

_____ antispasmodic, cooling, antiseptic, astringent

_____ estrogenic, calming, antiseptic, emollient, restorative, astringent

_____ moisturizing, soothing, regenerative

_____ germicidal, wound-healing, anti-inflammatory, antiseptic

_____ antioxidant, anti-inflammatory, stimulating, regenerative, antiseptic

_____ analgesic, circulation stimulant, cooling, calming, antiseptic

_____ decongesting, strengthening (capillaries), smoothing

_____ moisture-binding, soothing, softening, tightening, anti-inflammatory

_____ regenerative, astringent, calming

I	D	P	A	E	Z	B	D	B	I	A	N	N	J	Z
B	B	O	E	S	E	A	D	V	R	M	U	T	I	E
X	R	V	H	C	I	R	E	M	R	U	T	V	N	A
A	Q	I	H	A	T	U	T	Y	A	L	B	X	C	J
W	R	D	K	L	G	N	H	A	D	O	E	U	L	L
Q	O	W	L	O	E	C	I	K	E	H	Y	M	P	R
S	H	Z	Y	E	R	Z	U	M	R	T	C	I	O	S
U	P	V	A	V	A	Z	A	C	R	N	Y	S	J	N
U	M	O	U	E	N	E	Z	H	U	E	E	P	S	F
Z	A	R	H	R	I	J	M	B	H	M	P	U	A	W
B	C	L	Z	A	U	R	N	F	A	C	B	P	G	K
J	K	E	R	T	M	C	A	R	R	O	T	E	E	Z
B	D	I	E	F	O	P	Y	V	S	X	U	I	R	P
W	O	E	S	Z	A	Z	O	T	S	Y	X	X	W	M

20. Of the exfoliants used on problem skin, which is also antimicrobial? _____

21. Match the special agents for problem skin with their benefits.

    _____ glycerin   a. soothing, anti-irritant

    _____ oat flour   b. regenerative, hydrating, softening

    _____ glycoproteins   c. antimicrobial, reduces oil activity, dissolves keratin buildup

    _____ yeast beta-glucans   d. enhance cell metabolism

    _____ colloidal sulfur   e. emollient, soothing, moisturizing

22. Vitamins A, C, and E are all _____ . Vitamin _____ supports collagen synthesis, and vitamin _____ prevents tissue degeneration.

Discussion Questions

1. Advanced home-care treatments are often fairly expensive. Which overall benefits can you point out to clients as you recommend these specialized products?

2. How does knowledge of skin anatomy and basic chemistry help you sell advanced products?

3. Have you tried any of the advanced products described in this chapter? If so, describe your impressions of each.

CHAPTER 29
Methods of Hair Removal

Date _____

Rating _____

Text pages: 440–457

Introduction

1. Approximately how much money do consumers spend on hair-removal services every year?

   _____

TOPIC 1: Morphology of Hair

1. Match the following terms with their definitions.

   _____ hair shaft   a. soft, fine hair on a fetus

   _____ cuticle   b. swelling at the base of a follicle

   _____ lanugo   c. hard protein of which hair is made

   _____ hair follicle   d. outer layer of the hair shaft

   _____ keratin   e. tubular epithelial shield that surrounds lower part
                                 of hair shaft

   _____ medulla   f. middle layer of the three layers of the hair shaft

   _____ hair bulb   g. cavity in bulb of follicle that contains blood
                                 vessels and cells that nourish the follicle

   _____ cortex   h. innermost layer of hair shaft

   _____ dermal papilla   i. part of the hair that projects beyond the skin

2. Label the skin and hair structures in the following figure.

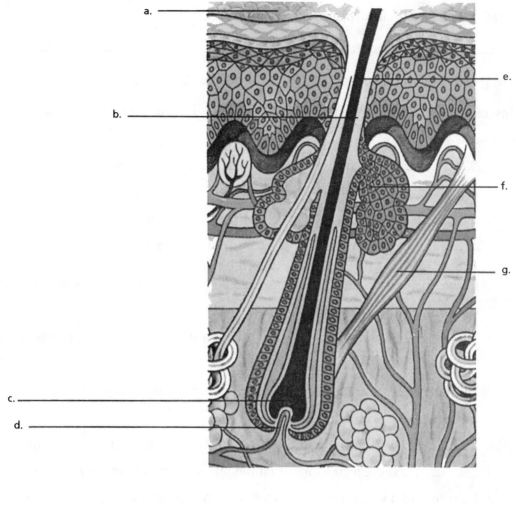

a. _____   e. _____

b. _____   f. _____

c. _____   g. _____

d. _____

3. The hair follicle, or _____ follicle, contains both a(n) _____ and the
_____ .

4. Generally, hair does not grow on the:

   a. _____

   b. _____

   c. _____

   d. _____

5. There are approximately _____ follicles per square inch on the face.

6. How are nutrients brought to the hair? _____

_____

7. When does hair formation begin? _____

_____

8. Hair growth occurs because of the activity of cells in the _____ layer.

9. Unscramble the words in the following list and use them to fill in the blanks in the following

sentences.

_____ sportichirhyes	_____ golteen
_____ gantace	_____ ennaga
_____ thuissirm	_____ choirt
_____ luvles riha	_____ grendonas

  a. In the final stage of hair growth, or _____ , the hair has reached full size and

  shows above the skin's surface.

  b. The term for excessive hair growth where hair does not normally grow is _____ .

  c. The fine, soft hair on the cheeks is a type of _____ .

  d. During the _____ stage of hair growth, the hair bulb pushes down, into the der-

  mis, and swells with cell mitosis.

  e. _____ is excessive hair growth on the face, arms, and legs, particularly in women.

  f. _____ is the regression, or falling out, stage of hair growth.

  g. Hirsutism in a woman may result when there is a glandular disturbance and excessive

  amounts of _____ are produced.

  h. The Greek word _____ means "hair."

10. Hair grows faster in a _____ climate.

11. Follicle size and function are _____ determined.

12. Causes of hirsutism other than hormones include:

  a. _____

  b. _____

  c. _____

  d. _____

  e. _____

TOPIC 2: Differences in Hair Growth and Characteristics

1. Which important functions does the hair perform in the body?

   a. _____

   b. _____

   _____

   c. _____

   d. _____

   _____

2. Generally, _____ and _____ hair is easier to remove than _____ hair, which is quite deep in the follicle.

3. Hair that tends to become ingrown is common among people from _____ and _____ .

4. Gray hair is more difficult to remove because _____ .

5. As much as _____ percent of a salon's income can come from epilation services.

TOPIC 3: Hair Removal

1. How do temporary and permanent hair removal differ? _____

   _____

   _____

2. Define the term *depilation*. _____

   _____

3. Define the term *epilation*. _____

   _____

4. Identify which of the following hair-removal methods is depilation, epilation, and permanent reduction by writing D, E, or P in the corresponding blanks.

   _____ shaving

   _____ sugaring

   _____ waxing

   _____ electrolysis

   _____ chemical depilatories

   _____ threading

_____ laser hair removal

_____ tweezing

5. Chemical depilatories should be used only after a _____ is taken for allergic reactions.

6. When tweezing, you should pull the hair in which direction? _____

7. _____ wax is applied to the skin, then covered with a strip of fabric that is immediately pulled away from the skin.

8. The temperature at which a solid substance liquefies is its _____ .

9. Additives to wax include _____ or _____ for sensitive skin and _____ for its soothing and antiseptic properties.

10. Identify the following skin-removal products using the following list of terms:

hot wax	roll-on system	sugaring
resin	soft wax	

_____ fluid, hydrosoluble, very thick depilatory

_____ melts at a lower temperature; easily removed with water

_____ available in sensitive creams or clear format for normal skin

_____ applied in several layers and picked up with fingers

_____ eliminates risk of cross-contamination

_____ very gentle, oil-soluble product melted at low temperature

_____ most efficient epilator for coarse, beardlike hair

_____ can be sticky and sometimes difficult to remove; best for longer hair

11. The _____ the wax, the more heat it requires to melt.

12. Wax must be _____ after each use.

13. Why do some estheticians prefer hard waxes? _____

_____

14. Generally, _____ wax is used on the back and legs, and _____ wax is used on the eyebrows, lips, and underarms.

15. Soft waxes have a _____ melting point than hard waxes.

16. Which type of wax must be removed immediately after it is applied: hard or soft? _____

_____

17. The benefit of roll-on wax is that it is _____ to use.

18. A method of hair removal that dates back to the ancient Egyptians is _____ .

19. The original sugaring recipe is a syrup made of sugar, _____ , and _____ .

20. Sugaring is used to remove _____ hair on the face, bikini area, underarms, legs, and back.

21. How is threading performed? _____

_____

_____

22. Laser and photo light hair removal is called _____ .

23. The only method of permanent hair removal is _____ .

24. Name and briefly explain the three methods of electrolysis.

    a. _____

    b. _____

    c. _____

25. Galvanic current transforms saline moisture inside the follicle into _____ , which destabilizes the follicle wall and allows the hair to be removed easily.

26. In thermolysis, an _____ current passes through a needle and coagulates the

_____ .

27. In the blend method, _____ and _____ currents are passed through the needle at the same time.

28. Electrolysis may be performed by _____ .

29. *Laser* is an acronym for _____ .

30. A laser is a beam of light, which is a form of _____ . This light penetrates into the _____ and the heat destroys the hair bulb in a process called _____ .

31. _____ colors absorb more light. For this reason, early-generation lasers were restricted for use on Fitzpatrick skin types _____ .

32. _____ lasers emit bursts of energy at extremely short intervals and shatter their target without allowing heat to build up. In this way the _____ or _____ is destroyed.

33. All laser devices must be approved by the _____ , and laser and photo light hair removal must be performed under the direct supervision of a _____ .

34. What are hair-growth inhibitors? _____

_____

_____

_____

TOPIC 4: Furniture and Accessories

1. Furniture for hair removal treatments should be _____ designed for both client and technician.

TOPIC 5: Tools and Supplies

1. Tweezers for waxing should be made of high-quality _____ .

2. Tweezers with a _____ are best for general tweezing; tweezers with a _____ tip are ideal for tiny hairs, ingrown hair, and difficult areas.

3. In terms of sanitation and convenience, _____ applicators are the best option.

4. If a stainless steel spatula is used to spread wax on larger areas, it must be _____ after use.

5. Tweezers and other stainless steel instruments can be disinfected in a _____ for 2 to 10 minutes.

6. List the purposes of prewaxing and postwaxing products and some examples of ingredients.

	Purpose	Ingredients
prewaxing solution	_____	_____
	_____	_____
		_____
		_____
postwaxing solution	_____	_____
		_____
		_____

7. Two popular types of strips are made of cotton and _____ , a fiberlike material that does not shed or stretch.

8. For each new client, place a clean sheet of _____ on the waxing table.

TOPIC 6: Sanitation

1. During hair-removal procedures, you should always wear _____ .

2. Any gauze or cotton that comes into contact with blood should be disposed of in a(n)

   _____ .

3. Slight bleeding or red bumps on the skin can be treated with _____ on a cotton
   pad.

4. Unless the manufacturer's instructions call for it, do not use _____ when waxing.

TOPIC 7: General Hair Removal (Waxing)

1. When removing the wax, pull the skin _____ and pull the muslin or pellon strip
   _____ the direction of hair growth.

2. List briefly the waxing contraindications and cautions for clients using the following:

   Accutane   _____

                                     _____

   Retin-A   _____

                                     _____

                                     _____

   antibiotics   _____

                                     _____

   birth control/   _____

     hormone replacement   _____

   blood thinners   _____

   autoimmune diseases   _____

     (lupus, AIDS)

   cancer therapy   _____

     (chemotherapy, radiation)

   diabetes, phlebitis   _____

open lesions (acne), cold sores, _____

    cysts, boils, growths, inflamed

    skin, sunburn, peeling/broken

    skin, cuts, moles, warts, active

    herpes virus

exfoliators (salicylic acid, _____

    AHAs, enzymes, scrubs, _____

    depilatory creams) _____

postcancer excess hair growth _____

_____

stimulants (alcohol, caffeine) _____

smoking _____

severe sun exposure, _____

    tanning beds _____

3. The following areas should never be waxed:

    a. _____

    b. _____

    c. _____

    d. _____

4. A first-time waxing client should always fill out a(n) _____ .

5. The first step in waxing the brows is _____ , followed by applying _____ to remove greasy residue or dirt.

6. Any thick or long hair should be _____ before applying wax.

7. Strip wax is applied beginning from the _____ to the _____ , while hard wax is applied in a _____ pattern.

8. Why should the muslin or pellon strip be pulled against the direction of hair growth? _____

_____

_____

9. Placing your hand quickly over an area after a wax strip has been pulled away _____

_____ .

Discussion Questions

1. If you have a male client who receives regular facials, how might you convince him to try hair-removal services for excessive hair on his back and shoulders?

2. Why is sanitation such an important concern in hair-removal treatments?

Word Review

anagen	hair bulb	hypertrichosis	photothermolysis
catagen	hair follicle	lanugo	telogen
dermal papilla	hair shaft	laser	vellus hair
electrolysis	hirsutism		

CHAPTER 30
Waxing Procedures

Date _____

Rating _____

Text pages: 458–483

TOPIC 1: Waxing the Eyebrows, Ears, Upper Torso, Legs

1. The most commonly requested hair-removal service is _____ .

2. Hair removal above the eye should generally be limited to the _____ and _____ _____ .

3. Hair on the earlobe or the top of the ear should be _____ before waxing.

4. Any hair inside the ear cavity should be removed only by _____ .

5. Hair on the body, such as on the back, shoulders, and bikini line, is best removed by _____ rather than shaving.

6. A leg-waxing service is divided into the following four parts:

    a. _____

    b. _____

    c. _____

    d. _____

7. Leg waxing generally lasts _____ weeks.

8. What is the basic bikini line? _____

_____

9. Why is Brazilian bikini waxing a controversial service? _____

_____

10. Removing ingrown hairs involves using a _____ to lift the embedded hairs and _____
_____ to remove them.

11. Using too much pressure to apply the strip may cause _____ .

12. How should the strip be removed after it is applied to the wax? _____

_____

TOPIC 2: Waxing Procedures

1. Client preparation for any facial waxing consists of the three following general steps.

a. _____

b. _____

c. _____

2. In the following graphic, draw three lines to indicate how the three points of the eyebrow are determined.

3. Explain how the guidelines for eyebrow shapes are adjusted for:

close-set eyes: _____

wide-set eyes: _____

_____

_____

4. After determining the eyebrow shape, you should _____ , then _____ the area thoroughly and allow it to _____ .

5. How do you test the temperature of the melted wax? _____

_____

6. The wax is applied from the _____ to the _____ of the orbital bone.

7. When the strip is placed over the wax, it is smoothed with _____ pressure, leaving about _____ of the strip free for pulling.

8. Immediately after removing the strip, _____ to block nerve pain.

9. Any minor hairs left after waxing may be removed by _____ .

10. The last step in the treatment is to apply _____

_____ .

11. If some wax falls on the eyelashes, apply a bit of _____ to the area with a cotton swab and roll it off with the wax.

12. Excess hair at the sideburn area and "peach fuzz" on the cheeks often become caked with _____ , and these areas are good areas for waxing.

13. Hard wax may be used in these facial areas, applied to the thickness of a _____ , and leaving a _____ that can be grasped for pulling.

14. For a client with coarse, deep-rooted chin hair, the best removal option may be _____ . Softer, fuzzy hair may be removed with _____ .

15. Hair inside the nose should only be removed by _____ .

16. Waxing the upper lip requires extra caution because the area is _____

_____ .

17. Is the upper lip waxed with hard or soft wax? _____

18. What are the disadvantages of shaving the underarm area?

a. _____

b. _____

_____

19. How does underarm hair grow? _____

a. How should strips be applied to the underarm? _____

_____

20. Both used wax and strips should be discarded in a(n) _____ .

21. The underarm area should be especially well cleansed before waxing, because it is a breeding ground for _____ .

22. When removing hair on the top of the forearm, ask the client to _____ _____ . To work on the back of the arm, elbow to shoulder, have the client _____ .

23. When working on loose or fleshy skin, be sure to hold the skin _____ so you do not irritate or injure it when removing the wax.

24. How should you position your arms when pulling strips or wax off the skin? _____ _____

25. The client should not expose any waxed areas to the sun or a tanning bed for _____ hours. The skin should also not be _____ or exposed to _____ water.

26. Because the back is very sensitive, you should first _____ a small area, then wax the back in small sections.

27. If you are waxing only the shoulder area, the client can be in which position? _____ _____ What about when waxing the entire back? _____ _____

28. Describe the three ways in which a client may be positioned for a bikini wax.

    a. _____

    b. _____

       _____

    c. _____

29. For a bikini waxing, _____ panties are most convenient.

30. In any waxing procedure, you must make sure the skin is _____ before you apply wax.

31. To soothe any discomfort, you may apply a _____ to sensitive areas.

32. If you spill wax accidentally on skin that you do not want to treat, use _____ to help remove it without pulling out any hair.

33. A client may use a _____ for cleansing to prevent ingrown hairs.

34. Retail products for ingrown hair contain _____ to keep hair soft.

Discussion Questions

1. Describe the measures you can take to ensure the least discomfort for the client during various waxing procedures, especially underarm waxing.

2. Explain how you would handle a client who is nervous about her privacy during a leg-waxing treatment.

CHAPTER 31
Color Theory, Facial Features, and Setup

Date _____

Rating _____

Text pages: 486–515

Introduction

1. How has makeup changed over the past decade or so? _____
_____
_____
_____

TOPIC 1: Color Theory

1. Define the following terms:

    primary colors   _____

    secondary colors   _____

    tertiary colors   _____
     _____

    complementary colors   _____
     _____

2. Identify the following colors as P=primary, S=secondary, T=tertiary, C=complementary, or N=none of the above.

    _____ yellow and violet

    _____ red-violet

    _____ blue

_____ violet

_____ red and yellow-orange

_____ blue-green

_____ blue and orange

_____ brown

_____ green

_____ red

3. With colored pencils or crayons, color and label the primary, secondary, and tertiary colors in the following color wheel.

COLOR WHEEL

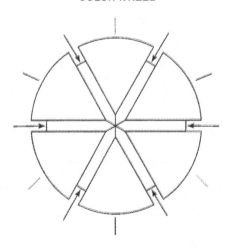

4. How are complementary colors used in makeup application?_____

_____

5. Match the following terms with their definitions.

_____ warm tones   a. blues, greens, violets, and grays

_____ shade   b. variation in a color achieved by adding white

_____ intensity   c. reds, oranges, salmon pinks, yellows, corals, and browns

_____ cool tones   d. lightness or darkness of a color

_____ tint   e. variation in a color achieved by adding black

_____ hue   f. another term for color

_____ value   g. degree of purity or brilliance of a color

6. Bright colors make an area appear _____ . Dark colors make an area appear

_____ .

7. How do the effects of warm tones differ from those of cool tones? _____

_____

8. What is makeup profiling? _____

_____

9. Developing a makeup profile requires observing the client's:

    a. _____

    b. _____

    c. _____

    d. _____

10. Identify the following skin-tone categories by their descriptions.

_____ olive skin with gold/yellow or orange/red undertones

_____ medium skin with pink or yellow undertones

_____ black skin with brown/yellow, brown/red, or brown/blue undertones

_____ fair, light skin with creamy or slightly pink undertones

TOPIC 2: Face Proportion and Shape

1. The facial shape that is referred to as the standard by which all other shapes are measured is the

_____ .

2. Identify the following basic facial shapes:

_____ _____ _____ _____

_____ _____ _____ _____

3. Divide the face into the three horizontal sections used to determine facial proportions.

4. Ideally, the space between the eyes should equal _____.

TOPIC 3: Facial Profile

1. List and briefly describe the three basic facial profiles.

a. _____

b. _____

c. _____

2. Color application on the cheeks should generally be limited to which area of the face? _____

_____

_____

_____

3. Contouring the face to achieve balance is done by _____ some features with light colors and _____ other features with darker colors.

4. Generally, the eyebrow should start at the _____ .

    a. One end of the eyebrow can be found by holding one end of a pencil _____ _____ and the other end _____ .

5. What are the four basic eyebrow shapes?

    a. _____

    b. _____

    c. _____

    d. _____

6. Using a light, cream-colored or pale-yellow colored pencil (or crayon) and a darker color (e.g., brown or dark blue), "correct" the eye shapes below by shadowing and highlighting.

deep-set eyes

small eyes

drooping eyes

protruding eyes

wide-set eyes

round eyes

hidden lids

close-set eyes

7. To sketch in missing eyebrow hairs, a good choice is a _____ pencil.

8. The most commonly corrected feature of the face is the _____ .

9. For purposes of makeup, the eye is divided into which three areas?

    a. _____

    b. _____

    c. _____

10. A well-proportioned eye area measures _____ from the base of the lashes to the crease line and _____ from crease line to eyebrow.

11. _____ eye shadow colors are always safe and fairly easy for the client to work with.

12. With dark and light colored pencils or crayons, shade or highlight the following nose shapes to balance them.

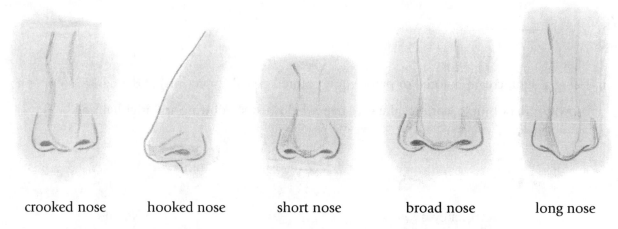

  crooked nose   hooked nose   short nose   broad nose   long nose

13. With horizontal lines, indicate on the following face the ideal proportions of the lips, nose, and chin. With vertical lines, indicate the ideal alignment of the corners of the lips.

14. How do soft and hard lips differ? _____

_____

_____

15. With colored pencils on the following, show how lipstick can be used to create the illusion of more balanced and well-proportioned lips.

Cupid's bow mouth
(pointed upper lip)

thin upper lip

straight upper lip

small mouth and lips

thin lower lip

fine lines around the lips

large, full lips

uneven lips

drooping corners

thin upper and
lower lips

1. List the five basic foundation types and the ways in which they are used.

a. _____

b. _____

_____

c. _____

_____

d. _____

_____

_____

e. _____

_____

2. The color of foundation and powder should be matched as closely as possible to the skin of

the _____ .

3. Describe briefly how to correct the following features with foundation:

wide jaw _____

_____

short nose _____

triangular face _____

_____

protruding forehead _____

double chin _____

narrow face _____

round/square face _____

_____

wide nose _____

_____

long, heavy chin _____

narrow forehead _____

_____

4. What are concealers? _____

_____

5. Concealer may be applied under foundation to _____ . It is applied over

foundation to _____ .

6. _____ is not designed to be applied directly to the skin.

7. The two types of powders are _____ and _____ .

8. Powders are used to _____ foundation and give it added _____ when the excess

powder is buffed off.

9. When natural oils come to the surface of the skin, the powder _____ them, giving the

skin a dewy quality.

10. If the client has dry skin or does not want much coverage, apply powder with a _____ .

If the client wants the foundation to stay on or stay true in color, apply it with a _____ .

11. What is flush, and how is flush color used? _____

_____

_____

_____

12. To determine a client's flush color, examine the:

      a. _____

      b. _____

      c. _____

13. What are glamour blush colors? _____

_____

14. Explain how flush and/or blush are applied. _____

_____

_____

_____

15. Fill in the following blanks from the following list of terms. (Note that not all terms are used.)

accent	eye shadow base	medium to darker
aged	fluff	neutral
angle	light	wet
eyes		

   a. Never use eye shadow that is the exact same color as the client's _____ .

   b. _____ shades of eye shadow are better for daytime wear.

   c. Using an _____ evens out the eye area and makes eye shadow stick and keep from creasing.

   d. You should apply a _____ shadow from the lash line to the area under the brow before adding a _____ shade.

   e. Use _____ brushes to apply shadow in larger areas and _____ brushes in smaller or crease areas.

   f. Eye shadow applied in the little fold some clients have at the outer edge of the eye makes the eyes appear _____ .

   g. Use _____ colors to highlight or complement unique features.

   h. Use _____ shadow as a liner instead of pencils if a client's skin is oily, a more refined line is needed, or you are lining over false eyelashes.

16. Pencils perform a number of functions and are used on the _____ , _____ , or _____ .

17. Using a white or blue pencil in the inner rim of the bottom eyelid can _____ _____ .

18. To keep the point of the pencil sanitary, _____ .

19. To help lipstick stay on the lips longer, use a pencil to _____ _____ .

20. Mascara _____ and _____ the appearance of the lashes.

21. There are several guidelines for applying mascara:

   a. For teens, use _____ mascara, for general purpose use _____ , and for clients with dark eyelashes use _____ .

b. _____ mascara makes lashes look fuller, and _____ applied to the tips makes them look _____ .

c. To avoid contamination, use a _____ to apply mascara.

d. Apply mascara to the _____ lashes first.

e. Should an eyelash curler be used before or after applying mascara? _____

22. _____ lipsticks tend to be more moisturizing, and _____ lipsticks adhere more to the lip.

23. To make lips look smaller, use a _____ lipstick shade; to make them look larger, use a _____ shade.

24. Correct any lip shape problems with a _____ .

25. List the steps of a lip color application that keeps lipstick from coming off.

    a. _____

    b. _____

    c. _____

    d. _____

    e. _____

26. Never apply lipstick directly to the client's mouth. Instead, scrape some off with a _____ and apply it with a _____ .

TOPIC 5: Makeup Tools

1. Fill in the following blanks from the following list of terms. (Note that not all terms are used.)

blush	gentle shampoo and	mops
brush	conditioner	pointed
comb	lip	powder
fan	liquid brush cleaner	sable
flat		

a. The largest makeup brush is used to apply _____ .

b. A _____ brush may be used to dust off eye shadow or blush powder that has flaked into an unintended area.

c. An eyebrow brush has a _____ on one end, used to separate lashes after mascara application, and a _____ at the other end, to remove powder residue from the brows.

d. _____ brushes are the stiffest brushes and are generally made of _____ .

e. For cleaning brushes immediately after use, a _____ , used only occasionally, is a good idea.

f. For longer-term use and your client's personal use, brushes should be cleaned weekly with a _____ .

g. Spongelike _____ are used to apply foundation.

h. _____ brushes are used to apply cleaners or to sweep off residues of pigment dropped where you do not want them to go.

i. _____ brushes are used to pat concealers or foundation onto the face.

2. Disposables include:

_____	for removing products from containers
_____	for applying mascara
_____	for applying lipstick
_____	for applying powder to the face
_____	for applying foundation and other cream-based products

3. To trim eyebrows or false eyelashes, use _____ .

4. Between clients, eyelash curlers should be cleaned by _____ .

5. You should not _____ a client's eyebrows on the day of a makeup application.

6. What are tabs? _____

7. When is white (transparent) eyelash adhesive preferred over black? _____

_____

_____

8. Why is a metal makeup palette preferable to the back of your hand for mixing makeup colors?

_____

_____

Discussion Questions

1. Which techniques can you use to avoid an overly made-up look?

2. How should the client's hair color affect your choice of makeup colors?

3. Why are some makeup products considered part of an overall skin-care regimen?

Word Review

complementary color	makeup profiling	shade	value
hue	primary colors	tertiary	warm or cool tones
intensity	secondary colors	tint	

CHAPTER 32
Makeup Applications

Date _____

Rating _____

Text pages: 516–537

TOPIC 1: Makeup Work Area

1. All makeup tools should be clean, sanitized, and kept in _____ containers.

2. When you take more product from a container, always use a _____ applicator.

TOPIC 2: Client Consultation

1. What are the three standard forms used during a makeup consultation?

   a. _____

   b. _____

   c. _____

   _____

2. The client should be scheduled to come in _____ minutes before the makeup session to complete the questionnaire.

3. Ask the client to come in _____ , so that you can get a visual sense of her own color selection and application technique.

4. The consultation offers a natural opening for _____ the client.

TOPIC 3: Basic Makeup Application

1. As part of the room setup, you should fill a bowl with warm water and soak _____ in it.

2. Number the following steps in a basic makeup application in their proper order.

   _____ apply concealer as needed

   _____ select and apply lipstick

   _____ apply day cream or moisturizer

   _____ optional step: apply false eyelashes

   _____ choose correct foundation and apply

   _____ apply toner over the entire face

   _____ apply mascara to bottom lashes, then top lashes

   _____ apply loose powder

   _____ lightly tweeze eyebrows if necessary

   _____ apply glamour blush

   _____ remove eye makeup and lipstick

   _____ fill in thinned areas in eyebrows with eyebrow pencil

   _____ apply cleanser to the face, beginning at the forehead, and rinse

   _____ apply eyeliner

   _____ apply eye shadow

3. Explain briefly how eye makeup should be removed. _____

   _____

   _____

   _____

4. How can lipstick be removed without smearing it on the face? _____

   _____

5. What is the best way to choose the correct foundation? _____

   _____

6. In which order are these eye shadows applied?

   _____ crease color

   _____ contouring

_____ base color

_____ accent color

7. If you want to achieve a smudged look with eyeliner, a _____ works best.

8. After applying mascara, you can separate the lashes with a _____ .

9. If artificial eyelashes are part of the service, mascara should be applied _____ the false lashes are.

10. Glamour blush and lipstick should enhance the client's _____ .

TOPIC 4: Choosing a Makeup Product Collection

1. Fill in each of the following blanks with a word from the following list:

branded	large	profit margin
consistency	marketing and support	specialty
custom-blended	materials	support
French	private label	

a. The most cost-effective way to select a makeup collection for a spa or salon is with a _____ line, because it offers a greater _____ .

b. With private label products, you have to produce your own _____ _____ .

c. _____ products are ideal for salons with a specific philosophy and system.

d. A drawback to custom-blended products is problems in _____ when duplicating a formula. They also require a _____ initial investment.

e. A _____ line supports other existing product lines such as skin care and hair care.

f. Branded lines offer the benefit of _____ through literature, education, and samples.

g. _____ branded lines are often very weak in color products required by women of color.

h. _____ lines are well suited as add-on items for marketing and special promotions.

TOPIC 5: Makeup Services

1. List the four basic makeup services.

   a. _____

   b. _____

   c. _____

   d. _____

2. Touch-up services are often tied into another salon service, such as a(n) _____ , a(n)

   _____ , or a(n) _____ .

3. For an evening look, increase the color on the _____ or _____ .

4. A makeup application takes about _____ minutes.

5. How is a makeup lesson generally conducted? _____

   _____

6. Wedding makeup is generally offered in two styles: one a _____ look and the other a

   _____ look.

7. What is another term for camouflage makeup? _____

8. Camouflage makeup can be used to conceal or normalize small skin imperfections as well as

   _____ .

TOPIC 6: Beyond the Basics

1. Generally, fashion trends run in cycles of _____ years.

2. List four ways in which you can keep up with makeup trends.

   a. _____

   b. _____

   c. _____

   d. _____

   _____

3. Savvy makeup artists make sure to _____ everything associated with the services they perform, such as makeup brushes.

Discussion Questions

1. What information do you need to know about a client before you can teach the client how to apply makeup?

2. If you were in charge of ordering makeup products for a salon, which of the four types of product collections would you choose—private label, custom blended, branded, or specialty? Why?

CHAPTER 33
The Value of Body Services

Date _____

Rating _____

Text pages: 540–555

Introduction

1. Why are pigmentation and wrinkling not as much a concern on hidden parts of the body as on the face? _____

_____

2. Back and scalp facials and full-body treatments are part of a more complete, _____ approach to skin care.

TOPIC 1: Who Can Do Body Treatments?

1. In some states, only _____ may perform body treatments.

2. To assure a more holistic and flexible approach and to avoid legal problems, it is recommended that professionals gain licensure in both _____ and _____ .

TOPIC 2: Concerns

1. An important issue for American clients is _____ during body treatments.

   a. How should these concerns be handled? _____

   _____

   _____

   _____

2. Two important hygiene and sanitation measures are making sure that _____ are

visible in all treatment areas and that estheticians _____ in front of clients.

3. Wet rooms must be _____ and _____ before a client enters.

TOPIC 3: Client Health

1. Before you perform any treatments on clients, you must be aware of their _____

_____ .

2. What is the purpose of the health history? _____

_____

TOPIC 4: Body Treatment Principles

1. What three elements do body and facial treatments share?

   a. _____

   b. _____

   c. _____

2. The greatest similarities between body and facial treatments are in _____ and the

   _____ .

3. The function of exfoliation in body treatments is to _____

   _____ .

4. Define the term metabolic stimulation. _____

_____

_____

5. List four of the more complex metabolic stimulation treatments.

   a. _____

   b. _____

   c. _____

   d. _____

TOPIC 5: Hydrotherapy

1. What is hydrotherapy? _____
_____

TOPIC 6: Service and Treatment Protocols

1. The _____ your client, the more body treatments you can offer either simultaneously or back to back.

2. Mixing and matching body treatments is known as _____ , the purpose of which is to _____ .

3. Giving a client too many treatments too soon may not be _____ .

4. _____ is the time a client has to relax after a stimulating treatment. The more _____ a treatment, the more relaxing time that is required.

5. Packages of overlapping services are attractive to clients and generally take _____ hours instead of an entire day.

TOPIC 7: Techniques for Body Treatments

1. The basic steps common to all body treatments are:

    a. _____

    b. _____

    c. _____

2. Fill in the following blanks from the following list of terms. (Please note that not all terms are used and that some terms are used more than once.)

AHAs	innermost	prone
body moisturizer	heavy cream	salt glow
brush machine	light oil	sideways
dry brushing	outermost	supine
friction		

    a. When preparing the table for two or more layered treatments, the _____ layer of materials represents the first treatment.

b. In the _____ position, the client faces down; in the _____ position, the client faces upward.

c. Generally, treatments begin with the client in a _____ position and end with the client in a _____ position.

d. Clients should be in the _____ position for the application of all slippery products.

e. _____ is a body exfoliation procedure designed to warm the body for many treatment protocols.

f. In the treatment called a _____ , the aggressiveness of the treatment depends on the ratio of salt to liquid solvent.

g. Many estheticians prefer mixing salt with a _____ , because the mixture allows for smooth application and has a nice slip.

h. Granular scrubs work by using _____ .

i. To enhance the exfoliating effect of granular scrubs, _____ are often added to the ingredients.

j. Another way to boost the effect of scrubs is by using the appropriate attachment on a _____ .

k. Body polishes must be followed by a _____ .

3. How are gommage products removed? _____

_____

4. Some gommages are formulated with an _____ , which helps dissolve cells.

TOPIC 8: Body Masks and Wraps

1. For consumers, what does the term body wrap describe? _____

_____

_____

2. Why do many spas not offer or recommend body wraps? _____

_____

3. What is a body mask? _____

_____

4. Shea butter wraps and milk and honey body masks are used to _____ the skin.

5. Seaweed and mud are often used in _____ treatments, which help the body

    _____ .

6. What are two main reasons a wrap is required over body treatments?

    a. _____

    b. _____

7. Algae are placed under the scientific category of _____ .

8. There are over _____ known species of seaweed.

9. List seven properties of algae that make them so beneficial in body treatments.

    a. _____

    b. _____

    c. _____

    d. _____

    e. _____

    f. _____

    g. _____

10. Name and define the two basic groups into which algae treatments are classified.

    a. _____

    b. _____

11. Identify the following seaweeds and place the letter of the corresponding type in the blank

    space: A=algae, G=green, BG=blue-green, BR=brown, or R=red.

    _____ strongest group for blood and metabolic stimulation

    _____ contains highly balancing emollient algae

    _____ rich in vitamins A, B, C, and E

    _____ aids in skin firmness and cell renewal

    _____ lichen moss is a subgroup

    _____ antioxidant and rich source of beta-carotene

    _____ has natural affinity for the human body

12. By law, muds and clays are tested for _____ .

13. Clay masks or packs are designed to _____ .

14. What is peat? _____

    _____

15. Moor mud is soothing and balancing and has _____ properties.

16. Identify the mud or clay by its description.

_____ rich in minerals; combined with paraffin for greater benefit

_____ fine powder used to draw, tighten, and tone

_____ rich in essential oils and minerals; used in masks and hydrotherapy

_____ high in minerals, magnesium, and potassium

TOPIC 9: Aromatherapy

1. The use of aromatherapy dates back to the ancient _____ and _____ .

2. What are essential oils? _____

_____

3. Essential oils work better in _____ than individually.

4. Essential oils benefit not only the skin but also the _____ , _____ , and

_____ .

5. List four ways in which essential oils are incorporated into a body treatment.

a. _____

b. _____

c. _____

d. _____

6. Essential oils are too strong to use undiluted, or _____ , and must be added to a blending oil.

7. Only a _____ should mix essential oils.

8. Identify the following essential oils as calming, stimulating, or detoxifying by writing C, S, or D in the appropriate space.

_____ lemon

_____ rose

_____ rosemary

_____ cinnamon

_____ chamomile

_____ thyme

_____ pine

_____ camphor

9. Identify each of the following treatments, then locate it in the word search puzzle.

_____ another term for granular scrubs

_____ treatment that makes use of essential oils

_____ performed with handheld brush, loofah, or loofah mitt

_____ obtained from bogs saturated with water

_____ application of a product over the entire body to firm or lightly exfoliate
the skin

_____ body exfoliation using product mixed with shower gel or light oil

_____ there are over 25,000 known species

_____ exfoliation process that may use xanthum gum as rolling agent

_____ includes Vichy showers as well as simple showers

_____ wrapping treatment used to treat cellulite

_____ type of seaweed; full of vitamins and minerals

K	D	B	B	O	M	F	B	A	Q	S	A	C	S
X	R	L	O	O	G	O	M	C	F	P	H	X	J
J	Y	E	Z	D	D	P	O	R	H	Y	L	W	O
Q	B	R	P	Y	Y	Y	M	R	D	Y	N	F	C
B	R	M	M	T	X	P	W	R	M	S	G	V	E
Q	U	A	R	K	X	M	O	R	R	U	M	D	G
X	S	T	F	D	K	T	L	L	A	Q	D	E	A
K	H	W	D	E	H	A	G	S	I	P	F	E	M
M	I	O	P	E	L	N	T	O	B	S	N	W	M
E	N	N	R	G	W	V	L	S	I	N	H	A	O
D	G	A	A	I	A	P	A	R	X	P	I	E	G
U	P	E	S	W	S	I	S	X	E	W	X	S	S
Y	P	A	R	E	H	T	A	M	O	R	A	Q	H
G	W	E	K	N	G	Q	I	S	J	L	T	G	W

TOPIC 10: Other Performance Ingredients

1. Performance agents, or _____ , are formulated to achieve a specific end result and are normally applied before _____ application.

2. What is the main goal of cellulite treatment? _____

_____

3. Why are serums not used more extensively in body treatments? _____

4. The last step in most body treatments is the application of a _____ .

Discussion Questions

1. People from other cultures often have fewer concerns about nudity and body treatments. Explain how body treatments for American clients are tailored to meet their concerns about modesty.

2. In what cases *must* a client be treated in a supine position? Why?

3. What "red flags" on a client's health form will alert you that certain body treatments may be contraindicated?

Word Review

activators	body wrap	metabolic group	salt glow
algae	detox treatments	metabolic stimulation	supine position
aromatherapy	dry brushing	posttreatment	vasodilation group
body polishes	hydrotherapy	stabilization	wet rooms
body mask	layering	prone position	

CHAPTER 34
Body Treatments

Date _____

Rating _____

Text pages: 556–573

TOPIC1: Body Treatments

1. In addition to exfoliation, all body treatments offer some level of _____ and

   _____ .

2. List the conditions for which all body treatments are contraindicated.

   a. _____

   b. _____

   c. _____

   d. _____

   e. _____

   f. _____

   g. _____

3. Female clients who are _____ should avoid excess heat and essential oils.

4. Claustrophobic clients should avoid _____ .

5. Masks, gommages, salt glows, and other treatments are contraindicated for clients with

   _____ .

6. Products used to condition the skin in body treatments are:

   a. _____

   b. _____

c. _____

d. _____

7. Number these steps in a remineralizing seaweed wrap in their proper order.

_____ wrap the client, who then rests for 10 minutes

_____ apply essential oils to the body or to the seaweed mask

_____ massage finishing lotion into client's skin

_____ apply warm seaweed mask, using blue-green, green, or red seaweed groups

_____ exfoliate, usually by dry brushing

_____ remove wrap with shower or hot towels

8. A detoxifying seaweed wrap uses _____ , which causes vasodilation and possibly sweating.

9. A detoxifying seaweed wrap also includes three detoxifying _____ and should contain some _____ seaweeds.

10. After a client is covered with warm mud, the client should be quickly covered with _____ and, if necessary, another _____ .

11. Clients receiving warm seaweed and mud wraps should be offered _____ .

12. What is the purpose of stabilizing time after a wrap? _____

_____

a. How long should stabilizing time last? _____

_____

13. Combining treatments such as a gommage exfoliation and a seaweed or mud treatment makes both treatments more _____ .

a. How does combining treatments benefit the esthetician? _____

_____

_____

14. What are the benefits of herbal wraps?

a. _____

b. _____

c. _____

15. A _____ is a special water heater used to heat the sheets for an herbal wrap.

16. The esthetician must be cautious when handling herbal wrap sheets, which are heated to
_____ degrees and weigh up to _____ .

TOPIC 2: Spot Treatments

1. The most common spot treatments are for the:

   a. _____

   b. _____

   c. _____

   d. _____

   e. _____

2. Bust treatments are designed to _____ .

3. Briefly explain the two different treatments referred to by the term *back treatment*.

   back facial: _____

   _____

   _____

   back treatment: _____

   _____

4. Number the following steps in a deep-cleansing back treatment in their proper order.

   _____ cleanse and disinfect

   _____ apply mud or oily skin mask for 10–15 minutes

   _____ disincrustation with galvanic current

   _____ apply freshener, light moisturizer, sunscreen

   _____ perform normal extractions

   _____ steam the back and treat with brush machine

   _____ remove mask with hot towels

   _____ exfoliate with deep pore cleanser

   _____ apply warmed freshener to remove cleanser residue

   _____ apply high frequency for 5 minutes

   _____ massage for 5–15 minutes

5. Which steps of a deep-cleansing back treatment are omitted for a relaxing back treatment?

   _____

6. How is exfoliation achieved in a deep-cleansing back treatment? _____

7. _____ is a genetically inherited condition that occurs in women. In severe cases, blood vessels, nerves, and other tissues are pressed against the skin by dense _____ .

8. Is it possible to cure cellulite? _____

9. What surgical procedures are used to help cellulite?

   a. _____

   b. _____

10. Cellulite treatments stimulate the circulation and metabolism through _____ , which helps the body get rid of _____ and _____ .

11. What steps can a client take to control cellulite?

   a. _____

   b. _____

   c. _____

   d. _____

12. In a cellulite spot treatment, after exfoliation an _____ serum or cream is applied, then a _____ mask and wrap are applied.

13. What is the focus of spa manicures and pedicures? _____

   _____

   _____

   a. What two steps in the usual manicure and pedicure are omitted in spa treatments?

      _____

      _____

14. Enhanced spa manicures and pedicures may include such treatments as:

   a. _____

   b. _____

   c. _____

15. Hand and foot treatments, including regular nail work, should not exceed _____ minutes.

16. An important contraindication for hand and foot treatments is the presence of _____

   _____ .

TOPIC 3: Paraffin

1. Paraffin has been used in hospitals to relieve the pain of _____ in the fingers and joints.

2. When used in a back treatment, paraffin may be applied over a _____ . It is often applied by first dipping _____ into it.

3. Paraffin applied to the hands, feet, or back should be covered with _____ .

TOPIC 4: Combination Services, Packaging, and Marketing

1. Whether or not you should combine services depends on the client's _____ .

2. Keep in mind that combining body treatments increases the _____ .

3. Combining a full-body wrap with _____ is not generally recommended because the client's feet become cool.

TOPIC 5: Body Massage

1. Fill in the following blanks with words from the following list. (Please note that not all terms are used.)

disinfected	one	psychological
effleurage	oxygen	sanitized
fluids	pattern	two
friction	petrissage	vibration
metabolic rate	physiological	warm
nutrition		

   a. Hands must be _____ before beginning massage.

   b. Hands and products must be as _____ as possible before they are applied to the body.

   c. Body massage uses mostly _____ movements.

   d. _____ and _____ are used to stimulate cellulite areas.

   e. Developing a regular _____ for massage and product application helps ensure consistency.

f. How many hands are used for massage? _____ How many are used to apply masks or wraps? _____

g. Massage provides both _____ and _____ benefits to the client.

h. Massage increases blood circulation and _____ .

i. Massage increases _____ and _____ to the body's organs and tissues.

2. Match the following Swedish massage movements, as used on the body, with their descriptions.

_____ petrissage

_____ percussion

_____ friction

_____ effleurage

_____ vibration

a. cupping, hacking, and slapping

b. movement originating from the shoulders as well as the hands

c. gentle but firm stroking

d. kneading movement

e. deeper, faster form of effleurage

3. What are the uses and benefits of the different massage movements?

effleurage _____

friction _____

petrissage _____

_____

percussion _____

vibration _____

4. The general order of a body massage begins with the client's _____ and ends with the _____ .

5. Before you include massage in your professional body treatments, it is your responsibility to

_____ .

6. Massage is not recommended for clients who are undergoing _____ or have the following conditions or diseases:

a. _____

b _____

c. _____

d. _____

e. _____

f. _____

g. _____

TOPIC 6: Shiatsu, Reflexology, and Similar Energy

1. Match the following terms with their definitions.

   _____ reflexology   a. energy pathways

   _____ chakras   b. nerve center triggers related to muscles, nerves, organs, and tissues in the body

   _____ meridians   c. massage and treatments based on division of body into energy zones

   _____ endorphins   d. treatment in which pressure is placed on specific points on the feet

   _____ Ayurvedic   e. body's own natural painkillers

   _____ shiatsu   f. energy zones in the body

   _____ motor points   g. finger pressure therapy

2. Meridians correspond to the _____ in the body and are believed to flow next to the _____ system.

3. When pressure is applied on the motor points, a natural _____ effect is produced through the release of _____ .

4. The concept of meridians originated in _____ .

5. In shiatsu, pressure is exerted on motor points by the _____ to activate energy to the motor point.

6. Performing shiatsu correctly requires an understanding of the concept of _____ discomfort.

7. How much pressure should be applied in shiatsu? _____

   _____

   _____

8. Pressure should come from the _____ rather than just the fingertips.

9. Who coined the term *reflexology*, and on which theory was it based? _____

   _____

   _____

   _____

10. Applying too much pressure or applying it incorrectly can lead to hand and wrist problems such as _____ .

TOPIC 7: Home Care

1. The purpose of selling body products is to _____ _____ .

2. Fill in the following blanks with terms from the following list. (Please note that not all terms are used.)

alkaline	detergents	metabolism
antibacterial agents	diuretic	nutrients
bath additives	higher	sloughing
cell renewal	liquids	sunscreen
creams	lower	

a. Professionally designed soap is not overly _____ , does not contain _____ that dry the skin, and has a _____ pH than grocery-store soaps.

b. Shower gel often has _____ that soften and condition the skin while cleansing.

c. Lotions are good for normal skins, while _____ are more beneficial for dry skins.

d. Hand lotions often contain _____ , while foot creams may contain _____ _____ for foot problems.

e. _____ are relaxing or detoxifying and can enhance the effectiveness of spa treatments.

f. Cellulite creams and serums stimulate the _____ and have a _____ effect.

g. Bust creams and serums work by accelerating _____ .

Discussion Questions

1. For a client who is already receiving regular facials, create a dialogue in which you explain additional benefits to be gained from body treatments.

2. What are your state's regulations concerning professional body massage?

back treatment

hydroculator

CHAPTER 35
Career Opportunities in Medical Esthetics

Date _____

Rating _____

Text pages: 576–581

TOPIC 1: Joining a Medical Team

1. Define the term *medical esthetics*. _____
   _____

2. In a cosmetic surgery, an esthetician may be in charge of the _____ , which is
   a separate department that generates its own profit.

3. Other functions an esthetician might perform in a cosmetic surgery are:

   a. _____

   b. _____

   c. _____

4. In a dermatology office, an esthetician's tasks might include assisting in _____ studies
   and trials.

5. An esthetician's responsibilities in an outpatient clinic revolve largely around _____
   _____ care.

6. A(n) _____ is often located near a hospital and serves patients from physician
   referrals.

7. Which services are offered in laser centers?

   a. _____

   b. _____

c. _____

d. _____

8. What is nonablative wrinkle treatment? _____

_____

9. In a _____ a patient may receive spa services and surgical procedures in a medical setting.

10. What is the purpose of a collagen injection? _____

_____

11. One task an esthetician may perform in a medi-spa is _____ , or machine massage for cellulite.

Discussion Questions

1. Is there a career in medical esthetics that appeals to you? Which one, and why?

2. What advanced training is required for various careers in medical esthetics?

3. What skills would be useful for an esthetician managing an ancillary profit center? For an esthetician working in an outpatient clinic? For an esthetician working with a cosmetic dentist?

Word Review

ancillary profit center   collagen injection   medical esthetics   nonablative

CHAPTER 36
Plastic and Reconstructive Surgery

Date _____

Rating _____

Text pages: 582–595

Introduction

1. The practice of using skin grafts in plastic reconstructive surgery dates back to around _____ _____ in _____ .

2. The term *plastic* in the phrase "plastic reconstructive surgery" means _____ .

3. _____ plastic surgery for the purpose of looking younger became routine in the twentieth century.

TOPIC 1: The Disciplines

1. Explain the difference between reconstructive and cosmetic surgery. _____

   _____

   _____

2. Match the following physician specialties with their general descriptions.

   _____ dermatologist

   _____ oral/maxillofacial surgeon

   _____ general plastic surgeon

   a. performs procedures on accident survivors and others with disfigurements

   b. performs plastic or cosmetic surgery on face and body

   c. specializes in diseases and disorders of the skin, hair, and nails

_____ reconstructive plastic surgeon   d. board certified in otolaryngology

_____ facial plastic surgeon   e. specializes in treatment of mouth and jaw

3. An _____ specializes in the treatment of the sinuses, throat, mouth, ear, and thyroid.

TOPIC 2: Facial Procedures

1. Using the clues, unscramble the following terms and write them in the spaces provided.

thoytmerdicy   ___ ___ ___ ___ ___ ___ ___ ___ ___ ___ ___ ___

Clue: face-lift

flimtini   ___ ___ ___ ___ ___ ___ ___ ___

Clue: rhytidectomy performed alone rather than in combination with other procedures

happystabrello   ___ ___ ___ ___ ___ ___ ___ ___ ___ ___ ___ ___ ___ ___

Clue: procedure that removes fat and skin from upper and lower eyelids

snopthilary   ___ ___ ___ ___ ___ ___ ___ ___ ___ ___

Clue: procedure that makes the nose smaller, larger, or straighter

polsottya   ___ ___ ___ ___ ___ ___ ___ ___ ___

Clue: procedure that flattens the ears

2. Which three things does a rhytidectomy accomplish?

a. _____

b. _____

c. _____

3. A rhytidectomy targets mostly the _____ .

4. The procedure performed on the lower eyelids to remove fat pads is called _____
_____ .

5. Laser resurfacing makes use of the power of _____ .

6. How do lasers smooth wrinkles in the skin? _____

_____

7. Explain how the two most commonly used lasers are employed.

carbon dioxide: _____

erbium: _____

8. Collagen _____ stimulates the growth of new collagen in the dermis.

9. Laser resurfacing is most effective on Fitzpatrick skin types _____ . On other skin types it may cause severe _____ changes.

10. For which conditions are trichloroacetic acid (TCA) peels particularly recommended?

a. _____

b. _____

c. _____

11. TCA is an alternative to laser resurfacing for Fitzpatrick skin types _____ .

12. The strongest chemical peel is the _____ peel. It has longer-lasting results but a longer recovery period than _____ .

TOPIC 3: Body Procedures

1. Using the clues, unscramble the following terms and write them in the spaces provided.

costipuloin	mullaibrantcis	vanobeltian
italingo	pharreestocly	yotecangasim
malsaptodibony	smatamaplym	

_____ procedure that reduces pockets of fat in areas that do not respond to diet or exercise

_____ surgery that enlarges, balances, or reconstructs the breasts

_____ breast implantation method that goes through the navel

_____ excessive development of the male mammary glands

_____ procedure that tucks and tightens fat deposits and loose skin in the abdomen

_____ eradication of veins with injections of saline or other solutions

_____ tying off extremely large or deep bulging veins

_____ wrinkle treatment using intense pulsed light

2. Breast implants may be put in place with the help of an _____ , a long tube with a lighted end.

3. Incisions for breast implants are made in the following areas:

    a. _____

    b. _____

    c. _____

    d. _____

4. Breast implants are usually filled with a _____ solution.

5. What are three health reasons for breast reduction?

    a. _____

    b. _____

    c. _____

6. The safest and most effective form of liposuction today is _____ .

7. In abdominoplasty, commonly called a _____ , the abdominal wall is strengthened and the waistline narrowed.

8. Botox is a _____ serum created from a _____ .

9. Botox works by decreasing a _____ ability to function.

10. Name some medical uses for botox.

    a. _____

    b. _____

    c. _____

    d. _____

11. What are the two main sources of animal collagen? _____

12. What is one routine but somewhat controversial source of human collagen? _____

13. List the uses for collagen fillers.

    a. _____

    b. _____

    c. _____

    d. _____

    e. _____

    f. _____

14. How are lasers used to treat spider veins? _____

_____

15. _____ phlebectomy is normally performed in a physician's office.

    a. In this procedure, bulging veins are removed with _____

       _____ .

    b. The patient must wear _____ for a short time after bandages are removed.

16. For the removal of skin tags, warts, small cysts, some skin cancers, and moles, _____

    _____ may be used.

17. Lasers have the ability to destroy hair in the _____ stage of growth.

18. The pulsed light in nonablative treatments are designed to stimulate _____ synthesis.

Discussion Questions

1. Botox treatments have become commonplace in recent years. What drawbacks have been associated with botox use? Conduct research into the topic if necessary.

2. What are the health benefits of breast reduction? Of abdominoplasty?

Word Review

abdominoplasty	endoscope	phlebectomy	sclerotherapy
areola	gynecomastia	reconstructive	transconjunctival
axilla	ligation	reconstructive plastic	blepharoplasty
blepharoplasty	liposuction	surgeons	transumbilical
(eyelift)	mammaplasty	rhinoplasty	method
collagen remodeling	maxillofacial surgeons	rhytidectomy	
cosmetic or aesthetic	otoplasty	(face-lift)	
surgery			

CHAPTER 37
Patient Profiles

Date _____

Rating _____

Text pages: 596–609

TOPIC 1: Patient Groups

1. List the five types of patients with which an esthetician is most likely to work.

    a. _____

    b. _____

    c. _____

    d. _____

    e. _____

2. Postoperative therapies that an esthetician might provide for a patient include:

    a. _____

    b. _____

    c. _____

    d. _____

3. Fill in the following blanks in the sentences from the following list of words. (Please note that not all words are used.)

access	injuries	nurse
counseling	intuition	physician
daily tasks	involved	referral resources
degenerative	mandatory	stabilized
frivolous		

a. When working with survivors of abuse, it is important not to become too _____ .

b. Always work in partnership with the _____ .

c. Do not ask patients about their _____ .

d. Do not offer _____ unless you are trained and authorized to do so.

e. Create a library of _____ to offer the patient.

f. You can help elderly patients overcome the feeling that cosmetic procedures are
_____ .

g. For patients with physical challenges, make _____ as easy as possible.

h. Remember that with _____ disabilities the condition may have worsened the next time you see the patient.

i. Make _____ easy for the patient, even if it means changing the room around.

j. If you have valid reasons for not wanting to perform a treatment on someone, honor your _____ and refer the client to a physician.

TOPIC 2: Pre- and Postoperative Care

1. The skin heals more quickly from plastic surgery if _____ has been improved beforehand.

2. A plastic surgery patient has a consultation first with the surgeon, then with the _____ .

3. During the consultation, you must determine if the patient is _____ , that is, if he or she will follow directions.

4. Why is proper home care so important?

   a. _____

   b. _____

   c. _____

5. Your plan for patients addresses products, treatments, and how you will _____ the patients to ensure they will follow all protocols.

6. List three attributes of the ideal candidate for elective surgery.

   a. _____

   b. _____

   c. _____

7. Patient education consists of instructing the patient with the necessary protocols to ensure a _____ .

8. Teaching by "show and tell" entails using both verbal and _____ information, having the patient _____ the information, and then reviewing it.

9. For visually impaired patients, use an _____ method of instruction.

10. How can you help a visually impaired patient with skin-care products? _____
_____

11. Because the medical environment can be strenuous, it is recommended that you find a support person or _____ to help you relieve stress.

TOPIC 3: Medical Documentation

1. All the information in a client's chart is _____ and available only to authorized personnel.

2. What does the acronym SOAP stand for?

   S _____

   O _____

   A _____

   P _____

3. Objective data consists only of what is seen, without a _____ being made by the esthetician.

4. Define the term *treatment protocol.* _____
_____

5. In medical offices, all office protocols and procedures must be contained in a _____
_____ manual.

6. _____ agents penetrate beneath the epidermis and are available by prescription only.

7. "Informed consent" means that a patient not only agrees to the treatment or procedure but also understands and accepts all _____ involved.

Discussion Questions

1. Which skills do you think an esthetician needs to work successfully with patients in a medical setting?

2. Imagine that a laser patient has come into your clinic complaining that one of the products in his home-care regimen is irritating his skin. Write your consultation with the patient in SOAP format.

Word Review

active agents   informed consent   protocols   SOAP

auditory   patient education

CHAPTER 38
Pre- and Postoperative Care

Date _____

Rating _____

Text pages: 610–621

Introduction

1. Conditioning in the preoperative phase includes:

    a. _____

    b. _____

2. The goals of conditioning in the postoperative phase are to:

    a. _____

    b. _____

    c. _____

    d. _____

3. In both preoperative and postoperative phases the skin must be protected from _____

_____ .

TOPIC 1: Procedures and Treatment Plans

1. The success of laser resurfacing depends greatly on the patient's willingness to _____

_____ .

2. What is included in a typical prelaser home-care kit?

    a. _____

    b. _____

    c. _____

    d. _____

    e. _____

3. In days 5–10 after laser surgery, the most important goal is to keep the skin _____

    _____ .

4. A postlaser kit typically includes copper peptide cream, used to _____ .

5. Presurgery protocols for rhytidectomy and forehead lift patients ideally begin _____ weeks before surgery.

6. General protocols are followed for rosacea patients, with the added use of _____ to reduce redness and swelling.

TOPIC 2: Treatments Defined

1. Define the term *manual lymphatic drainage (MLD).* _____

    _____

2. _____ is caused by excess water, protein, and waste in connective tissue.

3. The benefits of preoperatively applied MLD include:

    a. _____

    b. _____

    c. _____

4. MLD should *not* be performed on anyone with:

    a. _____

    b. _____

    c. _____

    d. _____

    e. _____

    f. _____

5. Estheticians are qualified to use only chemical peels that do not penetrate beyond the

    _____ .

6. AHA and BHA peels are also known as _____ because they are easy to perform and relatively inexpensive.

7. When applied before laser resurfacing, TCA peels, face-lifts, and eye and forehead lifts, the appropriate chemical peel enhances the skin's _____ .

8. Some chemical peels, such as glycolic and Jessner's, are capable of lifting superficial

_____ .

9. Chemical peels should *not* be given to anyone:

a. _____

b. _____

c. _____

d. _____

e. _____

f. _____

g. _____

h. _____

10. Microdermabrasion _____ built-up tissue and simultaneously _____ up the crystals and debris.

a. Microdermabrasion is often used in _____ management.

b. It can safely be used up to _____ before a surgical procedure.

c. Microdermabrasion has the advantage of stimulating _____ , which helps the skin heal faster.

d. Microdermabrasion is contraindicated for:

_____

_____

_____

_____

_____

e. Microdermabrasion is an excellent preparatory treatment for a _____ on arms and hands.

f. Benefits to the patient of using microdermabrasion are:

_____

_____

_____

_____

11. _____ is a cellulite treatment given before and after liposuction.

    a. Contraindications for this procedure are:

_____

_____

_____

    b. Benefits of this procedure for the patient are:

_____

_____

12. Ayurvedic and Swedish massage can be used preoperatively to _____ and postoperatively to _____ .

13. Computer imaging incorporates:

    a. _____

    b. _____

    c. _____

    d. _____

14. During computer imaging with a client, a split screen shows the patient's current image on one side and, on the other side, _____ _____ .

15. In the following chart, fill in the recommended preop and postop treatments for each procedure.

Procedure	Preop Treatment	Postop Treatment
face-lift/rhytidectomy		
eyelift/blepharoplasty		
forehead lift		
laser resurfacing		
liposuction		
breast augmentation		
breast reduction		
abdomectomy (tummy tuck)		

Discussion Questions

1. Explain the importance of maintaining and referring to specific guidelines for pre- and postoperative care.

2. Technology has contributed greatly to the advancement of skin care. What personal skills must an esthetician possess to make the best use of this technology?

Word Review

chemical peels   computer imaging   conditioning   endermology

CHAPTER 39
Camouflage Therapy

Date _____

Rating _____

Text pages: 622–629

Introduction

1. To camouflage means to _____ .

2. The same basic principles of _____ application apply to camouflage therapy.

3. Before deciding on a course of action, the esthetician must first determine if camouflage therapy is addressing the patient's _____ or _____ needs.

4. The darker a color, the more it _____ ; the lighter the color, the more it _____ .

TOPIC 1: Short-Term Use of Camouflage Therapy

1. Camouflage makeup has a _____ consistency than regular makeup.

2. An excellent way to teach a patient how to apply camouflage makeup is to _____

   _____ .

3. Because camouflage makeup application may be an emotional experience for the client, it is important that you show _____ .

1. Fill in the following blanks with terms from the following list. (Please note that not all terms are used.)

base	infection	tenth
bruising	mineral powders	3 weeks
clog pores	patted on	2–4 months
eye shadow	powder	yellow
hypertrophic	10 days–2 weeks	

   a. Makeup is allowed _____ after laser treatment, when the danger of _____ has passed.

   b. The erythema created by laser resurfacing can last _____ .

   c. To camouflage postlaser redness, the best makeup choice is sheer, inert _____ _____ , and the best color choice is _____ .

   d. Heavy makeup or powder should be avoided because it may _____ that have become more refined after laser surgery.

   e. Light layers of _____ are applied first, and then _____ is patted over redder areas.

   f. Postoperative condition after a rhytidectomy is characterized mostly by _____ .

   g. Sutures and staples are removed by about the _____ day after a rhytidectomy.

   h. Some face-lift scars are _____ or have a ridge; others are flat.

   i. When applying makeup to an eyelift patient, first apply _____ to cover the bruised area.

   j. After blepharoplasty, shadow may be applied on the incision after about _____ if it has healed sufficiently.

   k. Eye makeup remover should be _____ rather than pulled across the incision site.

2. If a person with a disfigurement seems angry or unhappy and not ready for camouflage treatment, it is best to _____ .

3. Camouflage therapy should *not* be performed on patients with:

   a. _____

   b. _____

c. _____

d. _____

e. _____

TOPIC 3: Micropigmentation: Permanent Cosmetic Makeup

1. Define the term *micropigmentation*. _____
_____
_____

2. Applying dye into the dermis was done by the _____ as early as 2000 B.C.

3. Name some types of reconstructive surgery in which micropigmentation is used to improve the patient's appearance afterward.

    a. _____

    b. _____

    c. _____

    d. _____

4. Permanent makeup is particularly useful for individuals:

    a. _____

    b. _____

    c. _____

    d. _____

    e. _____

5. Permanent makeup is applied in a _____ manner.

Discussion Questions

1. Which skills do you think are critical for anyone working with patients requiring camouflage therapy?

2. Explain the signs and symptoms of a patient who is not yet ready for the services of an esthetician.

3. How can an esthetician in a medical setting work most effectively with the physician? Which attributes do you think a physician would most appreciate in an esthetician?

American Academy of
  Micropigmentation

camouflage

micropigmentation

Society of Permanent
  Cosmetic Professionals

Multiple-Choice Test 1

1. Saponification is a process that:
   - a) introduces ions into the skin
   - b) occurs during disincrustation
   - c) has an antiseptic effect on the skin
   - d) is performed by sparking the electrode

2. Oily skin:
   - a) lacks oil
   - b) lacks lipid secretions
   - c) can also be dehydrated
   - d) is the same as sensitive skin

3. A purpura is caused by:
   - a) allergic reaction
   - b) chronic scratching
   - c) bacterial infection
   - d) bleeding under the skin

4. Fibroblasts are specialized cells that produce:
   - a) keloids
   - b) melanin
   - c) collagen
   - d) intercellular lipids

5. Antibodies are produced in the _____ system.
   - a) endocrine
   - b) immune
   - c) circulatory
   - d) nervous

6. Scowl lines may be removed by injecting Botox into the:
   - a) corrugator
   - b) orbicularis oculi
   - c) zygomaticus major
   - d) digastric muscle

7. The U-shaped bone at the front of the throat is the:
   - a) mandible
   - b) mastoid
   - c) hyoid
   - d) sphenoid

8. Stimulating motor points in the body induces:
   - a) increased energy
   - b) hormonal output
   - c) relaxation
   - d) follicular expansion

9. Only the process of sterilization can kill:

   a) HIV

   b) bacterial spores

   c) tuberculosis bacteria

   d) bacteria and viruses

10. The epidermis is made almost entirely of:

    a) keratinocytes

    b) desmosomes

    c) melanocytes

    d) ceramides

11. The valence shell is the:

    a) innermost ring of electrons

    b) shell of bound electrons

    c) most stable shell of electrons

    d) outermost ring of electrons

12. Essential amino acids must be included in the diet because the body:

    a) manufactures amino acids of inferior quality

    b) needs them to form beneficial micronutrients

    c) needs them to avoid arteriosclerosis

    d) cannot manufacture them

13. Abdominoplasty is:

    a) liposuction on the stomach area

    b) tucking and tightening of abdominal fat deposits and loose skin

    c) removal of the abdomen

    d) a chemical peel of the midsection

14. Betacarotene is:

    a) a provitamin

    b) the sunshine vitamin

    c) water soluble

    d) also called tocopherol

15. Of the following lipids, which contains vitamins A, E, and K?

    a) soybean oil

    b) sweet almond oil

    c) squalane

    d) orange roughy oil

16. If you accidentally drop wax on your client's eyelashes, you should:

    a) wash it off with warm water

    b) remove it with petroleum jelly

    c) remove it with wax solvent

    d) gently pull it off

17. Esthetic therapies may be performed on postoperative patients after about:

    a) 2 weeks

    b) 1 week

    c) 4 days

    d) 2 months

18. Antioxidants such as vitamins E and C protect the body from:

   a) bone abnormalities

   b) osteoporosis

   c) protein-synthesis disorders

   d) damage caused by free radicals

19. A 10-diopter lamp has:

   a) 10X power magnification

   b) 1X power magnification

   c) 100X power magnification

   d) -10X power magnification

20. Deep peels are performed with:

   a) phenol

   b) lasers

   c) TCA

   d) resorcinol

21. The unit used to measure the rate of flow of an electrical current is the:

   a) ohm

   b) ampere

   c) watt

   d) hertz

22. The flat sheet on a facial bed is draped over the:

   a) bare facial bed

   b) cotton towel

   c) fitted sheet

   d) light blanket

23. For an esthetician's purposes, skin type is determined primarily by:

   a) secretions

   b) blood tone

   c) amount of melanin

   d) the presence of allergies

24. Endermology is a treatment given before and after:

   a) laser resurfacing

   b) liposuction

   c) abdomectomy

   d) breast augmentation

25. The makeup color commonly used to camouflage redness in the skin is:

   a) yellow

   b) brown

   c) beige

   d) green

26. One of the primary purposes of obtaining and recording a client's health information is to:

   a) gather appropriate products for the service

   b) monitor the client's progress

   c) inform the client of the procedures planned

   d) avoid harming the client

27. An acne papule:

   a) is red with a white center

   b) is an inflammatory lesion

   c) can easily be felt under the skin

   d) darkens when exposed to oxygen

28. Clients taking prescription keratolytics may receive:

    a) hard-setting masks

    b) gentle massage

    c) waxing treatments

    d) chemical exfoliation

29. A skin analysis begins:

    a) when the client arrives, still in makeup

    b) after light cleansing is finished

    c) after all makeup has been removed

    d) when the skin is observed through a loupe

30. On the Fitzpatrick Scale, skin type VI:

    a) tends to be more reactive to the environment

    b) is the most resistant to solar elastosis

    c) is more tolerant of deep chemical peels

    d) has the least melanin

31. The completion phase of a facial includes:

    a) deep massage

    b) mask application

    c) application of a night cream

    d) application of moisturizer and sunblock

32. The massage technique that stretches the limbs and applies pressure on acupressure points is:

    a) acupressure

    b) shiatsu

    c) Swedish massage

    d) lymph drainage

33. Close-set eyes can be corrected in part by:

    a) lining the eyes from corner to corner

    b) applying a darker shade to the lids

    c) applying dark shadow toward the nose

    d) blending shadow outward

34. The most important elements of a minifacial are:

    a) massage and mask

    b) skin analysis and massage

    c) deep cleansing and mask

    d) deep cleansing and electric treatment

35. A male client is likely to prefer:

    a) rose-scented products

    b) creams that leave a glossy look

    c) foaming cleanser

    d) as many products as possible

36. Ayurvedic treatment is based on three mind and body types, also called:

    a) polarities

    b) doshas

    c) meridians

    d) pressure points

37. A salt glow performed on the hands or feet is an example of:

a) reflexology

c) a detox treatment

b) a spot treatment

d) aromatherapy

38. The percentage of sales generated from retail in a successful spa is about _____ percent.

a) 15–25

c) 30

b) 50

d) 40–45

39. An example of a subjective symptom is:

a) severe rash

c) stinging

b) erythema

d) lesions

40. Rosacea is:

a) most common in Fitzpatrick types IV–VI

c) treated with antiyeast medication

b) more common in men than women

d) triggered by cold weather

41. Zinc oxide and titanium oxide:

a) are chemical sunscreens

c) are more likely to irritate the skin

b) absorb and neutralize UV rays

d) are made of earth pigments

42. One problem with hydrocortisone is that it:

a) causes breakouts and aggravates flares

c) can mask other symptoms

b) is stored in the body, where it is toxic

d) is highly comedogenic

43. The positively charged particles in an atom are:

a) neutrons

c) protons

b) electrons

d) quarks

44. The role of an emulsifier in a skin care product is to:

a) moisturize the skin

c) keep oil and water blended

b) act as a vehicle

d) reduce surface tension

45. The function of a hydrator is to:

a) attract water to the skin

c) neutralize free radicals

b) remove sebum from the skin

d) treat alipidic skin

46. Ingredients in advanced skin care products that help strengthen the immune system and stimulate the metabolism are:

a) liposomes

c) polymers

b) microsponges

d) polyglucans

47. The term *rhytids* refers to:
   a) surgery on loose skin   c) wrinkles
   b) softening of the bones   d) vitamin A derivatives

48. The technical term for sun poisoning is:
   a) polymorphous light eruption   c) Favre-Racouchot
   b) solar poikiloderma   d) solar elastosis

49. Telangiectasias are treated in the salon with products containing:
   a) masoprocol   c) hyaluronic acid
   b) ceramides   d) vitamin K and bioflavonoids

50. The single most effective antiaging product is:
   a) moisturizer   c) exfoliant
   b) sunscreen   d) AHAs

51. Irritant reactions:
   a) can affect any skin type   c) occur slowly rather than immediately
   b) affect only certain individuals d) are an immune disorder

52. Sclerotherapy is performed to remove _____ veins.
   a) small   c) medium-size
   b) bulging   d) spider

53. Under the Wood's lamp and the skin scope, the color brown indicates:
   a) sun damage   c) normal healthy skin
   b) dehydrated skin   d) thin skin

54. The major cause of mottling, chloasma, and other hyperpigmentation is:
   a) sun exposure   c) aggressive exfoliation
   b) stress   d) hormone therapy

55. The causes of acne do *not* include:
   a) sex hormones   c) retention hyperkeratosis
   b) hereditary factors d) chocolate and greasy food

56. Western medicine is considered:
   a) homeopathic   c) chiropractic
   b) ayurvedic   d) allopathic

57. A hospital-grade disinfectant must be able to kill:

a) hepatitis viruses and tuberculosis bacteria

c) mold and mildew

b) herpes and hepatitis viruses

d) syphilis and tuberculosis bacteria

58. The functions of skin include:

a) relaying nerve impulses

c) regulating body temperature

b) giving shape to the body

d) bearing weight

59. The most important product(s) an Asian client can use is:

a) moisturizer

c) sunscreen

b) clay masks

d) chemical exfoliant

60. Gommage should not be used on clients with:

a) oily skin

c) open comedones

b) sensitive skin

d) hyperpigmentation

61. The system that works with endocrine glands to monitor and maintain other body systems is the _____ system.

a) cardiovascular

c) nervous

b) respiratory

d) immune

62. The most common cosmetic enzymes are derived from:

a) fruits or vegetables

c) meat protein

b) digestive bacteria

d) seaweed

63. A truly holistic regimen:

a) uses only natural ingredients

c) focuses on the mind, body, and soul

b) incorporates only spiritual practices

d) combines machine and hands-on therapies

64. A client with a history of herpes simplex may receive exfoliation and other stimulating treatments if:

a) only physical exfoliation is used

c) sanitation measures are practiced

b) the client takes preventive antiviral drugs

d) there are no active lesions

65. The most common allergen in cosmetics and skin care products is:

a) physical sunscreens

c) color agents

b) fragrance

d) essential oils

66. Eye cream or gel helps to relieve dark circles by:

    a) lightening the skin around the eye   c) suppressing melanin production

    b) stimulating microcirculation   d) exfoliating debris
       in the area

67. The hair bulb contains an oval-shaped cavity filled with tissue, called the:

    a) dermal papilla   c) hair root

    b) medulla   d) arrector pili

68. The regression stage of hair growth is called:

    a) telogen   c) catagen

    b) lanugo   d) anagen

69. In laser hair removal, the laser light passes harmlessly through the skin and destroys the:

    a) nucleus of the white blood cell   c) nerve cells

    b) sebaceous glands   d) hemoglobin of the red blood cell

70. Hard wax should be applied:

    a) with gloved fingers   c) to the thickness of a dime

    b) in a figure-eight pattern   d) with a fabric strip

71. Jessner's solution is a liquid solution of lactic acid, salicylic acid, and:

    a) AHA   c) water

    b) acetone   d) resorcinol

72. Protons and neutrons together compose:

    a) a negative charge   c) the nucleus

    b) the valence shell   d) a covalent bond

73. Electrolysis may be recommended for the removal of _____ hair.

    a) nasal   c) bikini-line

    b) ingrown   d) deep-rooted, coarse facial

74. An annular lesion looks like a:

    a) target   c) map

    b) ring   d) snake

75. When you add white to a color, you create a(n):

    a) tint   c) shade

    b) intensity   d) hue

76. The galvanic machine:

    a) produces chemical reactions   c) converts direct current to oscillating current

    b) has a thermal effect on the skin   d) stimulates lymphatic drainage

77. A diamond-shaped face is widest at the:

    a) temples   c) cheekbones

    b) jawline   d) chin

78. The eyebrow shape that can give the face a surprised look is:

    a) straight   c) Asian

    b) arched   d) curved

79. Comedolytic products:

    a) cause comedones and pustules   c) aggravate redness and itching

    b) loosen comedones   d) lighten the skin

80. Upon arrival for a makeup session, the client fills out a:

    a) makeup profile   c) skin analysis form

    b) makeup diagram   d) confidential makeup questionnaire

81. The issue of greatest concern in today's spas is:

    a) privacy   c) sanitation

    b) taxes   d) liability

82. Exfoliation is performed on the body to:

    a) increase product penetration   c) assist in layering

    b) calm sensitive skin   d) stimulate the metabolism

83. Finishing lotions, creams, or oils:

    a) may smell like mud or algae   c) tighten and tone the skin

    b) are applied at the end of a   d) are applied after massage
       treatment

84. Detox treatments help the body eliminate:

    a) sebum   c) toxins

    b) alcohol   d) perspiration

85. A combination of two body treatments usually takes:

    a) 50 minutes   c) 25 minutes

    b) 90 minutes   d) 1 hour

86. When pressure is applied to motor points, the body releases:
    a) endorphins
    b) adrenaline
    c) hormones
    d) sebum

87. An ancillary profit center is a(n):
    a) clinic treating only hands and feet
    b) dermatology office making a profit
    c) outpatient clinic
    d) profit-generating department in a medical office

88. Clients suffering from rosacea should avoid:
    a) antioxidants
    b) grapeseed and green tea extracts
    c) vasodilators
    d) antibiotics

89. Nonablative wrinkle treatments stimulate:
    a) collagen in the dermis
    b) sebum in the epidermis
    c) lipid barrier function
    d) keratinocyte production

90. Langerhans are immune cells found in the:
    a) epidermis
    b) dermis
    c) papillary layer
    d) lymph nodes

91. Otoplasty is performed on the:
    a) nose
    b) ears
    c) lips
    d) eyes

92. Collagen remodeling is a procedure that:
    a) moves collagen from one area of the face to another
    b) selectively removes collagen
    c) stimulates new collagen growth in the dermis
    d) injects collagen in specific areas

93. A legal document stating that the patient agrees to a procedure and accepts all risks involved is called a(n):
    a) SOAP form
    b) intake form
    c) treatment protocol
    d) informed consent form

94. Skin treatments before surgery serve to:
    a) make the surgeon's job easier
    b) shorten surgery time
    c) condition the skin to heal
    d) put the patient at ease

95. The massage movement used mainly to stimulate sebum production is:
    a) effleurage
    b) percussion
    c) vibration
    d) petrissage

96. Comedonal acne:

    a) occurs mostly in adults

    b) must be referred to a physician

    c) is a rare form of acne

    d) is the most common form of acne

97. Drugs related to vitamin A are known as:

    a) corticosteroids

    b) antibiotics

    c) retinoids

    d) antihistamines

98. The federal agency responsible for overseeing workplace safety is:

    a) EPA

    b) NIH

    c) FDA

    d) OSHA

99. Before applying hard or soft wax, you should make sure the area is:

    a) dry

    b) warm

    c) wet

    d) powdered

100. Sensitive skin should be cleansed with products that:

    a) are high in detergent

    b) are nonfoaming or low-foaming

    c) do not contain lipids

    d) contain emulsifiers

Multiple-Choice Test 2

1. Physiological changes in the skin occur over time mainly in the:
   - a) epidermis
   - b) fatty layer
   - c) dermis
   - d) connective tissue

2. Ligaments are types of:
   - a) hyaline cartilage
   - b) bones
   - c) skeletal muscle
   - d) connective tissue

3. During the first week after eye-lift surgery, a patient's home-care regimen must include:
   - a) copper peptide cream
   - b) camouflage makeup
   - c) ice
   - d) hydrating eye cream

4. Micropigmentation is *not* used to create or restore:
   - a) a receding hairline
   - b) pigment loss
   - c) eyebrows
   - d) eyeliner

5. Mineral oil and petrolatum are *not*:
   - a) comedogenic
   - b) biologically inert
   - c) emollient
   - d) safe for the skin

6. Qi, or chi, is a(n):
   - a) healing tea
   - b) needle therapy
   - c) massage therapy
   - d) energy system

7. The jellylike fluid that fills the spaces between collagen and elastin fibers is:
   - a) adipose
   - b) ground substance
   - c) mucocutaneous fluid
   - d) eleidin

8. Metro-gel cream is used as a(n):

a) antioxidant

b) topical antibiotic

c) anti-inflammatory

d) hydrator

9. Coenzyme Q10 is a(n):

a) anti-inflammatory agent

b) hydrator

c) antioxidant

d) delivery system

10. The system that helps maintain the body's water and chemical balance is the _____ system.

a) skeletal

b) digestive

c) endocrine

d) urinary

11. Mast cells in the immune system produce:

a) antigens

b) T-killer cells

c) eleidin

d) histamine

12. Loose powder is applied from:

a) the container

b) the palm of the hand

c) a facial tissue

d) a palette

13. The skull consists of _____ bones.

a) 8

b) 26

c) 14

d) 22

14. Before a remineralizing mud wrap, the client is first:

a) warmed

b) massaged

c) cleansed

d) exfoliated

15. Increased sebum production may be caused by:

a) hormonal changes

b) dirt

c) AHA use

d) *P. acnes* bacteria

16. The ideal candidate for elective surgery is someone who:

a) is elderly

b) can afford it

c) has realistic expectations

d) is incapacitated by the disorder

17. Pus-forming bacteria called streptococci cause:

a) tuberculosis

b) herpes

c) pneumonia

d) strep throat

18. A French dermatologist, Dr. Jacquet, developed a massage technique that is particularly beneficial:

    a) for very oily skin   c) after laser treatments

    b) for dehydrated skin   d) for clients with rosacea

19. Antibiotics are drugs that kill:

    a) fungi   c) bacteria

    b) all pathogens   d) viruses

20. Manual lymphatic drainage uses light rhythmic movements to:

    a) detoxify tissues   c) stimulate hormonal flow

    b) remove dead surface cells   d) dehydrate the skin for surgery

21. A hemangioma is a:

    a) type of micropigmentation   c) hypertrophic scar

    b) very large mole   d) red birthmark

22. Infections caused by fungi are known as:

    a) bloodborne infections   c) aseptic infections

    b) mycoses   d) proliferative diseases

23. Macronutrients needed by the body include:

    a) proteins, fats, and fiber   c) proteins, carbohydrates, and fats

    b) carbohydrates, proteins, and water   d) starches, simple sugars, and fiber

24. Flexors are muscles in the:

    a) forearms   c) shoulders

    b) upper back   d) upper arms

25. Fatty esters:

    a) are derived from plant and animal fats   c) have been exposed to hydrogen

    b) usually end in -*ate* on ingredient lists   d) protect the skin from UV rays

26. It is best not to apply talcum powder after waxing because it:

    a) becomes damp and sticky   c) contains fragrance

    b) may cause an allergic reaction   d) takes too much time

27. A Wood's lamp is used during a skin analysis to:

    a) diagnose skin disease   c) magnify the skin

    b) illuminate skin problems   d) treat pigmentation disorders

28. The usual time between leg waxings is:
    a) 4 to 6 weeks
    c) 1 to 2 weeks
    b) 1 month
    d) 2 months

29. Alphahydroxy acids:
    a) loosen chemical bonds between keratinocytes
    c) slow lipid production
    b) suppress melanin replacement
    d) gently strip the stratum corneum

30. Disincrustation should be applied to areas of the skin that:
    a) are deeply wrinkled
    c) are dry and flaky
    b) are alipidic
    d) have more sebaceous secretions

31. A watt measures:
    a) the rate of flow of an electrical current
    c) a material's resistance to the flow of electric current
    b) the rate at which current is delivered
    d) the rate of electrical energy consumption

32. The main difference between cocoon and noncocoon draping is that noncocoon draping:
    a) adds a bed warmer
    c) adds a flat or fitted sheet
    b) omits head protection
    d) omits the light blanket

33. Dehydrated skin:
    a) is the same as alipidic skin
    c) lacks water
    b) is the same as sensitive skin
    d) lacks oil

34. In a patient's chart, treatments and protocols are included in the:
    a) subjective data
    c) assessment
    b) objective data
    d) plan

35. Arteriosclerosis may be prevented with a diet rich in:
    a) trans fatty acids
    c) omega-3 fatty acids
    b) polysaccharides
    d) triglycerides

36. AHAs are used to treat hyperpigmentation because they:
    a) block the sun's UV rays
    c) remove keratinocytes containing melanin
    b) suppress melanin production
    d) bleach the skin

37. Electrical treatments are contraindicated for:
    a) clients with acne
    c) clients who are pregnant
    b) clients taking birth control pills
    d) clients taking preventive antiviral drugs

38. Tweezers with pointed tips are particularly useful for removing:
    a) very long hair
    b) curly hair
    c) lanugo
    d) ingrown hair

39. The drug called Accutane:
    a) stays in the body a long time
    b) produces few skin side effects
    c) is quickly flushed from the body
    d) is available over-the-counter

40. Properties of algae do *not* include:
    a) skin-restructuring proteins
    b) assistance in cell renewal
    c) antioxidant properties
    d) blood vessel constriction

41. Acnegenic substances:
    a) help dry up acne lesions
    b) are beneficial for clients with rosacea
    c) have no known side effects
    d) cause follicular inflammation

42. Erythemic skin is defined as skin that:
    a) turns red easily
    b) is thick and nonreactive
    c) hyperpigments easily
    d) is prone to breakouts

43. Foundation color should match the color of the:
    a) neck
    b) palm of the hand
    c) cheeks
    d) inside of the mouth

44. Under a Wood's lamp, dehydrated or dry areas of the skin appear:
    a) whitish
    b) dark brown
    c) bright or neon yellow
    d) blue to deep purple

45. The main difference between a quick cleanse and a full cleanse is the addition to the latter of a(n):
    a) physical exfoliant
    b) AHA or BHA
    c) foaming cleanser
    d) facial freshener

46. Petrissage should *not* be used on:
    a) fleshier parts of the face
    b) skin with pustules
    c) thick, leathery skin
    d) oily skin

47. For male clients who have just shaved, you should avoid using:
    a) cleansing milks
    b) AHAs
    c) masks
    d) all of these products

48. The most important element of effectively selling products is:

   a) explaining the features of the products

   b) educating clients on how the products benefit them personally

   c) selling in bulk whenever possible

   d) explaining research and development

49. Atopic dermatitis is:

   a) a genetic condition

   b) worse in summer months

   c) a form of rosacea

   d) treated with antifungal medication

50. Paraffin masks:

   a) can be applied under mud or seaweed

   b) are removed before they cool

   c) are applied more thinly in winter

   d) infuse nutrients into the skin

51. Mohs' micrographic surgery is performed on:

   a) skin cancers

   b) telangiectasias

   c) chickenpox scars

   d) spider veins

52. Home-care compliance is very important because it:

   a) counteracts surgical results

   b) expedites the healing process

   c) makes the program less expensive for the client

   d) means less time and effort for the esthetician

53. Actinic lentigines, patches, and plaque are examples of:

   a) primary lesions

   b) secondary lesions

   c) malignant lesions

   d) vascular lesions

54. Corticosteroids are:

   a) prescription drugs for cystic acne

   b) OTC drugs for lightening the skin

   c) hormones that help relieve inflammation

   d) any drugs derived from vitamin A

55. The acid mantle:

   a) is made of sebum and sweat

   b) varies in pH between 4.5 and 7.2

   c) is a type of buffering agent

   d) is unaffected by product pH

56. Chemical peels may safely be performed on clients with:

   a) moderate rosacea

   b) cold sores

   c) infectious disease

   d) Fitzpatrick skin types I–III

57. Free radicals are:

   a) stable oxygen molecules

   b) used in antioxidants

   c) unstable oxygen atoms

   d) beneficial to the lipid cell membrane

58. The seventh most common cancer in the United States is:
   a) colon cancer
   c) lung cancer
   b) melanoma
   d) basal cell carcinoma

59. Alphahydroxy acids (AHAs) help reverse the visible signs of sun damage by:
   a) relayering epidermis cells
   c) providing an occlusive barrier
   b) destroying free radicals
   d) stimulating melanin production

60. Atoms are made up of:
   a) electrons and protons
   c) a nucleus and quarks
   b) protons and neutrons
   d) electrons and quarks

61. In the condition known as dermatographism:
   a) capillaries are distended
   c) the skin burns quickly
   b) the skin reacts to product fragrances
   d) the skin swells easily

62. Allergic reactions may be treated with:
   a) topical hydrocortisone
   c) hot towels
   b) oral hydroquinone
   d) hyaluronic acid

63. To reinforce the barrier function on sensitive skin, you may use:
   a) AHAs
   c) clay masks
   b) lipid ingredients
   d) stimulants

64. Anaerobic bacteria such as *P. acnes*:
   a) feed on sudoriferous material
   c) are killed by exposure to oxygen
   b) form cysts
   d) are extremely inflammatory

65. Grade 4 acne is distinguished from other grades by the presence of:
   a) deep nodules and cysts
   c) inflamed areas
   b) severe erythema
   d) papules and pustules

66. Compared to Caucasian skin, black skin:
   a) is oilier
   c) has fewer elastic fibers
   b) has more and larger sebaceous glands
   d) is more susceptible to skin cancer

67. Estheticians are allowed to remove cells:
   a) in the basal layer
   c) in the dermis
   b) from the stratum corneum
   d) below the stratum granulosum

68. The betahydroxy acid most commonly used in the salon is:
    a) Retinol
    b) trichloroacetic acid
    c) salicylic acid
    d) butylated hydroxyanisole

69. Pacinian, Meissner, and mucocutaneous corpuscles are all types of:
    a) nerve endings
    b) blood cells
    c) adipose cells
    d) immune cells

70. The enzyme papain comes from:
    a) cows
    b) papaya
    c) pineapple
    d) citrus fruits

71. Bones are attached to other bones by:
    a) epithelial tissue
    b) ligaments
    c) rete pegs
    d) tendons

72. A therapy that concentrates on the head and spinal column is:
    a) shiatsu
    b) shiodara
    c) Reiki
    d) craniosacral massage

73. Regenerative ingredients help:
    a) increase lipid barrier function
    b) stimulate hormonal activity
    c) regenerate fibroblastic activity
    d) renew sebum production

74. An alkaline reaction is achieved with the:
    a) positive pole during ionization
    b) negative pole during ionization
    c) positive pole during disincrustation
    d) negative pole during high-frequency treatment

75. Which of the following is a phyto extract?
    a) elastin
    b) squalane
    c) hypericum
    d) hyaluronic acid

76. New hair is formed when nutrients are brought to the base of the bulb by:
    a) melanocytes
    b) blood vessels
    c) sebaceous glands
    d) keratinocytes

77. Permanent hair removal involves the destruction of the:
    a) papilla
    b) hair bulb
    c) follicle
    d) arrector pili

78. Combining a primary and secondary color next to each other on the color wheel produces:

   a) complementary colors

   b) a tertiary color

   c) a secondary color

   d) a primary color

79. Olive tones are characteristic of:

   a) dark Hispanic skin

   b) light Caucasian skin

   c) medium Asian skin

   d) light Asian skin

80. The product that lifts impurities and dead cells from the skin during a facial is the:

   a) cleanser

   b) freshener

   c) mask

   d) ampoule

81. Cheek color should not be applied lower than the:

   a) base of the nose

   b) chin

   c) middle of the nose

   d) lip area

82. Underarm hair must be waxed carefully because:

   a) waxing may cause ingrown hairs

   b) the hair grows in different directions

   c) it is potentially injurious to the client

   d) the hair tends to be deep rooted

83. The most cost-effective type of makeup line to begin with is a:

   a) specialty line

   b) private label line

   c) branded line

   d) custom-blended line

84. The three basic elements of a spa body treatment do *not* include:

   a) electric treatments

   b) skin treatment

   c) cleansing and exfoliation

   d) body stimulation

85. When you apply slippery products during a body treatment, the client should be:

   a) sitting

   b) prone

   c) lying on his or her side

   d) supine

86. Fiber is a carbohydrate needed by the body for:

   a) proper digestion

   b) energy for bodily functions

   c) the breakdown of proteins

   d) the transport of nutrients

87. An effective shiatsu treatment involves:

   a) heavy pressure on motor points

   b) pressure exerted with the fingertips

   c) comfortable discomfort

   d) deep but short-lived pain

88. An imbalanced atom:

a) has lost or gained an electron

b) has no outer ring of electrons

c) does not carry an electrical charge

d) has more protons than neutrons

89. An esthetician must possess advanced knowledge of major malpractice and liability insurance to work in a(n):

a) medi-spa

b) hospital

c) cosmetic dentistry

d) independent clinic

90. High-frequency current:

a) changes polarity 100 times per second

b) produces chemical changes

c) produces thermal or heat effects

d) oscillates 5,000 times per second

91. Every product used in the salon or spa should have a(n):

a) warranty

b) opaque container

c) MSDS

d) OSHA registration number

92. Collagen injections are:

a) usually plant derivatives

b) administered by estheticians

c) used to remove age spots

d) given to fill wrinkles

93. Transconjunctival blepharoplasty removes fat pads from the:

a) upper eyelids

b) jawline

c) lower forehead

d) lower eyelids

94. The motor nerve that controls the muscles involved in chewing is the _____ nerve.

a) cervical

b) fifth cranial

c) seventh cranial

d) buccal

95. Laser resurfacing is not recommended for patients with:

a) darker skin pigments

b) deep wrinkles

c) acne scarring

d) skin cancer

96. Primary lesions that appear as pinpoint red spots and are a result of trauma are called:

a) excoriations

b) palpable nodules

c) vascular macules

d) petechiae

97. An example of a contagious disease caused by bacteria is:

a) warts

b) molluscum contagiosum

c) tinea pedis

d) cellulitis

98. A Botox injection:

    a) improves a muscle's ability to function

    b) decreases a muscle's ability to function

    c) slowly dissolves small muscles

    d) increases muscle volume

99. Wax used in a hair removal service must be:

    a) recycled

    b) cleaned and reused

    c) given to the client

    d) discarded in a hazardous waste container

100. Over-the-counter ingredients approved for topical use on acne include:

    a) benzoyl peroxide

    b) prednisone

    c) hydroquinone

    d) hydrocortisone